'The transition to general management can be thorny, but Kaiser, Pich and Schecter make it both accessible and enjoyable. By letting us see through the lenses of three fictional leaders taking on new roles, they bring the journey to life, letting us feel both the growing pains and also the rewards. By the end, you will know these characters intimately, cheering them on when they succeed, shouting at them when they stumble, and smiling along with them as they acquire the practical skills and personal wisdom essential to becoming a general manager in today's global world.'

**Laurence Applebaum, Executive Vice President, Women's Tennis Association**

'In *Becoming a Top Manager*, Kaiser, Pich and Schecter cleverly address the three vital parts of the transformation: managing the business, managing others, and, perhaps most fundamentally, managing oneself. They also integrate the views of many who have attended their programs and successfully applied the lessons in their own careers. The result is a highly engaging, highly readable book that should be mandatory for anyone preparing to take this important step in their professional journey.'

**Fulvia Aurino, Brand General Manager, Estée Lauder and Tom Ford Beauty, Italy**

'By creating three fictional characters as chaperones on the journey, Kaiser, Pich and Schecter present the complex, largely unfamiliar world of general management with insight, empathy, and, in the end, inspiration. Anyone about to undertake this critical step in their career path will benefit enormously from reading *Becoming a Top Manager* and applying its lessons.'

**Martijn Bödeker, Managing Partner, CATALPA GmbH & Co. KG**

'*Becoming A Top Manager* asks and answers all the right questions when it comes to cultivating senior leaders! Kaiser, Pich and Schecter know exactly what it takes to make this journey from functional leader to GM. They outline a path fraught with complexity, but they don't sugar-coat any part of it. So if you're racing down the road to general management, make this book required reading – and doing.'

**Hal Gregersen, Executive Director of the MIT Leadership Center and co-author of *The Innovator's DNA***

'In *Becoming a Top Manager*, Kaiser, Pich and Schecter skilfully and cleverly address the three vital pieces of this transformation: managing the business, managing others, and, most important of all, managing oneself. You will not read a book that addresses the transition to general management in a more astute and engaging way.'

**Ricardo Ferrero, Global Marketing Lead, Baker Hughes**

'A must-read for those who aspire to become successful GMs. Kaiser, Pich and Schecter have done an excellent job of articulating the essence of general management in a compelling, inspiring and entertaining way.'

**Wopke B. Hoekstra, Partner, McKinsey & Company and member of Dutch Senate**

*'Becoming a Top Manager* is essential reading for anyone making the transition from functional leader to general manager. Readers will immediately relate to and learn from the fictional GMs presented within while being entertained and inspired by their experiences.'

**Roger Benson, Cloud & Mobility Multinational Sales Director, Intel EMEA**

'This book hits a powerful nerve in our world of change. Kaiser, Pich and Schecter brilliantly show how to transform into a top manager by not only managing the business, but also managing others, and, perhaps most crucially, managing oneself.'

**Lutz Finger, Director of Data Science & Engineering, LinkedIn**

*'Becoming a Top Manager* is critical reading for those transitioning to general management or seeking to do so. The stories of the three fictional GMs allow one to really experience the transformation, supported by a unique combination of insights and acumen from the authors and their former students – and all built upon the fundamental objective of creating value.'

**Ross Evans, Group Manager, Exploration Appraisal & Development, Origin**

*'Becoming a Top Manager* is a witty, thorough, no-nonsense guide to the tough reality of managing a business, managing others and – most difficult of all – managing oneself. In the journeys of these three fictional GMs, you will surely spot yourself more than once. Keep this book handy!'

**Laura Nemaric, Head of Corporate Treasury & Insurance Asia, Solvay**

'Integrating the experiences of many who have attended their programs, Kaiser, Pich and Schecter explain, in a practical and relatable way, how to tackle the key challenges managers in transition must inevitably confront. By introducing three fictitious managers on similar journeys, the authors have devised an unforgettable tool for offering wisdom, flagging pitfalls and enabling success in the next phase of your professional career.'

**Arnaud van Oers, CFO, IHC Asia Pacific**

'Many books have been written on leadership development and transition, usually with a topical dissection of the attributes that need to be modified, changed or improved. Most of these books lack a regard for the intangible realities of operating as a leader, particularly concerning the struggles in learning how to elevate one's horizon, consider value to the company before the department and forget about what one learned as a functional expert. *Becoming a Top Manager* uniquely captures and addresses these challenges by following three new GMs in very real situations that force them to reshape their behaviors, mindsets and priorities.'

**Greg Bunker, Global Business Director, Dow Chemical**

'*Becoming a Top Manager* is compelling because it defies easy categorization. It is a rock-solid business book blended with inspirational fable. It offers both deep insights from its authors as well as illuminating comments from their former students. It is a frank throwing back of the curtain mixed with an encouraging pep talk for those embarking on the complex transition to general management. Read this book.'

**Veit Dengler, CEO, NZZ Mediengruppe**

'Take your time reading *Becoming a Top Manager*. Be open to its teachings. Absorb the information it provides. Make it part of your own journey and adapt it to your personal situation. Kaiser, Pich and Schecter illuminate how to truly become a top manager – and how to position yourself to help those around you.'

**Frank Legters, Director Business Unit, Regional and Urban Environment, Royal HaskoningDHV**

# Becoming a Top Manager

Tools and Lessons in Transitioning to General Management

**Kevin Kaiser, Michael Pich and I.J. Schecter**

**JB JOSSEY-BASS™**
A Wiley Brand

*Library of Congress Cataloging-in-Publication Data*

Kaiser, Kevin, 1964–
  Becoming a top manager : tools and lessons in transitioning to general management / Kevin Kaiser, Michael Pich, and I.J. Schecter.
    pages cm
  ISBN 978-1-118-85857-8 (hardback)
  1. Executive ability.   2. Chief executive officers.   3. Management.   I. Pich, Michael T.   II. Schecter, I. J., 1971–   III. Title.
  HD38.2.K35 2015
  658.4'2–dc23

                                                                          2014038165

A catalogue record for this book is available from the British Library.

ISBN 978-1-118-85857-8 (hbk)
ISBN 978-1-118-85856-1 (ebk) ISBN 978-1-118-85855-4 (ebk)

Cover Design: Wiley
Cover Illustration: © kraphix/shutterstock.com

Set in 12/16pt ITCGaramond by Aptara Inc., New Delhi, India
Printed in Great Britain by TJ International Ltd, Padstow, Cornwall, UK

*We would like to dedicate this book to the thousands of participants of our executive programmes who have inspired us, motivated us and taught us much of what we know about what it takes to become a top manager and how to do it well.*

# Contents

# Acknowledgements

Numerous people helped us make this book a reality, beginning with Rosemary Nixon of Wiley, who first discussed with us the possibility of basing a book on the content of INSEAD's Transition to Management Programme (formerly the International Executive Programme) and worked diligently with us to find the right structure and shape for the manuscript. Thanks also to the rest of the global Wiley team for taking the book all the way to the finish line, including Kathe Sweeney and Ashton Bainbridge for shepherding it through the early stages, Jenny Ng for helping fine-tune it over the course of several months and Holly Bennion for overseeing the entire process, which anyone who has ever written a book knows is neither simple nor quick.

We are extremely grateful to Katherine Philips-Kaiser, who first proposed the idea of crowd-sourcing the content for the book and whose company, AmphiMedia, created and managed the interactive platform that was essential to making this project work. AmphiMedia also did an outstanding job of coordinating all matters relating to the participants and their contributions.

We are also grateful for the financial support of the ABN Amro Managing for Value Research Fund at INSEAD, which covered various costs related to this project.

Thank you to Moriah Productions in Singapore for planning and shooting the videos for that interactive platform, and to the actors who brought to life our fictional general managers, along with the accompanying cast of characters who gave voice to their mentors, sounding boards and foils.

Lastly, we are indebted to all of those who took time out of their busy lives and daily schedules to watch our fictional GMs in action and to provide the invaluable commentary, insights and anecdotes that give the book its true breadth and scope. Our contributors represent 18 different nationalities (including many who have spent time as expatriates) and a wide range of industries, functional backgrounds and roles. It is thanks to the input of this diverse group that we can confidently say our discussion of what it takes to become a successful general manager in today's global world transcends cultures and borders. You have our sincerest gratitude.

# Introduction

Functional leaders promoted to executive positions often find themselves lost at sea – unfamiliar not only with the responsibilities surrounding their new role but unsure of the skills and tools necessary to execute them successfully. The marketing manager promoted to partner; the communications lead moved up to the boardroom; the unit head who suddenly finds himself at the executive table. Individuals in such positions tend to quickly discover that the knowledge and capabilities that allowed them to thrive in their previous job have little bearing on the new one, and that a whole new set of skills – or rather, a whole new way of thinking – is suddenly required. They realize that to deliver their new mandate they must change. But how?

We decided the best way to answer this question would be to pose it to past participants of our executive education programmes, a broad mix of people from different backgrounds, industries, companies and geographies with one thing in common: they are somewhere on the new learning curve of what it means, and what it takes, to become a successful general manager. We asked this community to participate in the project via an interactive online platform through which they would watch videos of our three fictional general managers in action[1] – general managers created to represent a fair cross-section of role, industry, background, gender, experience

---

[1]The videos can be viewed at www.wiley.com/go/topmanager. See *About the Website* section for more details.

and personality – and then, in response to specific questions we provided, offer comments, observations and stories of their own related experiences.

We were delighted both by the enthusiastic response from so many willing contributors who took time out of their jobs and lives to watch the videos and provide comments, and by the depth and diversity of the insights and reflections they offered. These insights and reflections not only provided great context for the chapters that follow, they also allowed us to identify 10 key success factors that we feel will help guide others in making a similar transition from functional to general management. We present these 10 themes below, which you will see repeated throughout the book.

## Key Success Factors for Transitioning to General Management

Being an effective general manager requires the same thing today as it will require tomorrow: the willingness to lead, the openness to learn and an unwavering commitment to creating long-term value. The transition to general management is a change indeed, and it requires serious mental and emotional effort. Frequently, it represents a shift away from everything one has known in the past, and often entails the unlearning of lessons one has spent years trying to make second nature. Moving from a task-oriented role to a role of managing the tasks of others (management) and then to general management (where one is now responsible for managing the managers) involves significant changes in scope and comprehension.

Among the most difficult of the changes required by moving from a role of management of task-oriented people to managing the managers is the complexity of the jobs of those you are now charged with managing. When managing people with relatively clearly defined tasks, it is not overly risky to characterize success and failure within those tasks as delivery against a set of clearly defined indicators. However, a manager's role is far more complex than can be easily summarized by a set of indicators, no matter how clear or concrete.

The success of a manager includes delivery on multiple dimensions, each of which is imperfectly captured by concrete indicators, and which, when viewed together, are extremely difficult to measure in any straightforward way. For this reason, to assess and motivate the performance of managers, the general manager must be capable of seeing beyond the concrete indicators, which might summarize 'what' the manager accomplished, to assess 'how' and 'why' the manager delivered against them. The general manager must be capable of assessing whether delivery against the concrete indicators might have been at the expense of the long-term health of the company. While this big-picture view is difficult to explain and nearly impossible to measure, there are key success factors that we feel will help any general manager achieve the task.

## 1.  Questions are more important than answers

Successful functional managers often attribute their success to the knowledge and experience they gained in their previous functional role. Having become accustomed to having the answers, they experience great difficulty transitioning to a role that relies more on asking good questions. A general manager cannot have all the answers. He or she must instead learn to ask the right questions of his or her managers to assess how well they are managing the business.

If your people are simply waiting to be told what to do instead of playing an active role in problem-solving, then you have misunderstood your role as general manager. It is virtually impossible to imagine a business situation in the modern world in which the general manager knows what each person in his or her charge needs to do in order to succeed. Nor is it feasible that the GM knows which indicators will hit which levels by which date while the business is achieving long-term value creation. Instead of telling people what to do, or what to deliver by which date, the GM must work to ensure that people are actively asking the right questions. And the surest way to prevent your people from asking the right questions and contributing to the ongoing adaptability and problem-solving of your organization is to start telling them what to do instead of asking how you can help.

## 2.   Trust is key

When people look upward within the organization, they see a boss who has the power to overrule, embarrass or fire them. For this reason, their natural reaction to any person above them in the hierarchy is a combination of admiration (hopefully) and fear (unfortunately). As a functional manager you may have been the boss, but people could identify with you because you shared a functional identity and you were tasked with looking out for the interests of that functional area.

As a general manager, you no longer share this functional identity with those below you. Worse, you may have to make decisions that may not be seen as being in the best interests of the functional area you previously led. To ensure that everyone continues to speak openly and honestly to you as you move up the ladder, you must demonstrate fairness, openness and genuine respect. The honest input and feedback from those 'below' you is the key to success in your general management role, which means you must be conscious of behaviours that will compromise their willingness or ability to provide it. If they fear your authority, they will quickly shut down, but if they know you respect and value them, they will be forthcoming in the manner you need them to be for your own success. This trust can take years to earn, but can be lost in an instant.

## 3. Beware of your expertise

As mentioned, successful functional managers often attribute their success in moving up through the organization to the functional expertise that has to date propelled them forward. While this expertise may drive success and confidence, it may also prevent proper appreciation of the relevance of other areas in the company. As one moves up into a general management role, the ability to see and prioritize all areas of the business becomes key, yet the natural reliance on one's comfort zone may inhibit, or completely mask, this ability.

In addition, there is evidence that humans selectively focus on and recall data that supports their assumptions, which means our biases may increase, rather than decrease, as we become more knowledgeable on a topic. As a result, our expertise in a particular business function may simply strengthen incorrect presumptions and, worse, by building unfounded confidence, close our minds to the willingness to incorporate new data.

This effect is exacerbated by the tendencies of those below us in the hierarchy to agree with those above, further enhancing our misplaced confidence and solidifying our mistaken assumptions, especially if reinforced by those who have moved even further up the ladder.

## 4. Value is not earnings. Or market share. Or share price. Or ...

Moving into general management means expanding your scope on two key dimensions: (1) from short-term to long-term thinking; and (2) from a single area of responsibility to the impact on the entire organization. The concept of managing for value incorporates both dimensions, and is distinct from the tendency, especially for lower levels of management, to focus on narrow indicators that do not capture the performance implications for the entire organization or short-term targets that cannot incorporate the long-term impact of any decision.

We define the value of an organization as the present value of the expected future free cash flows discounted at the opportunity cost of capital. This concept is explained in detail in a recent book by one of the authors, *The Blue Line Imperative: What Managing for Value Really Means*. The expected future free cash flows are not simply those as estimated by management; they also incorporate unseen effects in other areas of the business, and in the future. For this reason, any estimate of value is by definition incorrect. The process of continuous learning is needed to ensure steady improvement in estimation in order to reduce the risk of value-destroying decisions.

The new general manager needs to resist the temptation to over-simplify the job by choosing to define success by narrowly defined, short-term performance indicators, and must instead maintain integrity by focusing on the long-term, organization-wide impact of any act or decision. The only way to expect those below you to do this is to demonstrate it yourself.

## 5.   Business is about serving customers

Every decision in business must be oriented around serving customers, and doing so in a way such that the organization makes enough money to support its continued health. Your organization does not seek this goal in isolation. Other companies are trying to serve your customers with similar products or services, and any success of theirs will come – to some degree – at your expense. Survival depends upon having a sustainable competitive advantage in the ability to serve customers while making money. Any discussion not focused on this customer-driven, efficiency-oriented perspective is one that needs to be reframed.

## 6.   Bias has no place in sound decision-making

It is well known that the human brain tends to follow mental processes which make use of shortcuts resulting in a variety of different
biases. These biases show up in the way we search for and select
data. They also affect the way we make decisions. (One example
is that we often have a bigger aversion to losses than attraction
to gains. Another is that, when making decisions in teams, we are
susceptible to considerable influence from others.) Finally, these
biases can inhibit our ability to learn. For example, we have an
easy time giving ourselves credit for successes, but we tend to find
excuses for our failures rather than deriving important lessons from
them. The GM must be conscious of these biases and be vigilant in
mitigating their impact – by forming diverse teams, soliciting independent opinions, collecting broad data sets, reframing questions,
and assigning and rotating the role of devil's advocate, among other
techniques.

## 7.   Morale counts for everything

The general manager doesn't really *do* anything. Rather, he or she
is responsible for managing the managers: those who do tasks and
manage others who do other tasks. If your people are not excited,
motivated and determined to come to work, to continue to learn
and adapt, and to drive decisions and actions to continuously re-
establish the business's competitive advantage and use it to create
and capture value, then you are not succeeding as a general manager. Use regular feedback to assess whether your style is motivating
individual members of your team, and always search for solutions
to maintain high morale.

And remember, in spite of the pressures of business, people like to
have fun. Look for opportunities to release pressure and build team
morale through activities such as innovation competitions, brainstorming exercises with prizes for the best ideas, and team-building
exercises oriented around problem solving.

## 8.  Success depends on teamwork

In addition to building morale, a GM must ensure that ongoing communication is taking place between team members to minimize siloed thinking, reduce inconsistencies and avoid conflicting efforts, which undermine overall efficiency and effectiveness. We work in teams to accomplish tasks one person cannot achieve alone. But there is a difference between a high-performing team and a low-performing one, and this difference is the GM's responsibility.

To achieve high performance, the team must have trust across all parties, a shared respect for the different roles, a common objective (creating long-term value) and regular communication. The general manager must be vigilant in ensuring these elements are in place, and are continuously reinforced and transparent to all.

## 9.  Learning comes from trust and fairness

The challenge of business – to deliver value to the customer more efficiently than the competition – is unrelenting. In order to continuously build the competitive advantage that allows the business to achieve this goal, all members of the team need to be involved, motivated and working in a coordinated way. Moreover, they must always be searching for new, innovative and creative ways to do it as the world – consumer preferences, regulatory rules, the competitive landscape, the technological frontier, the macroeconomic environment, and so on – continues to change around them.

This continuous learning can take place only if all members of the organization perceive fairness in all dealings and a sense of collective trust both in one another and in the decision-making process itself. The GM must always seek opportunities to reinforce these pillars and must, with equal diligence, watch for behaviours that undermine them.

## 10.   'Practice time' is critical

We learn through failure and the conscious effort to reflect on it, so that we can modify the process or adopt new techniques to improve. Musicians, athletes and others recognized for displaying high levels of performance in a particular area all go through a similar learning process: practice, feedback, reflection and coaching. These high-performing individuals are diligent and deliberate in practice, and in maximizing the learning from experimentation, so that their 'best' becomes subconscious and can be instantly deployed come game time.

The general manager must actively look for ways to incorporate experimentation and learning through feedback into day-to-day business. Only he or she is able to provide this space by encouraging learning, supporting experimentation and avoiding behaviours which hinder either one. Learning occurs when the GM builds experimentation into the business in such a way that potential losses due to failure are less than the expected value of the learning to be achieved. The GM who can build into the day-to-day management of the business a culture of continuous learning through small-scale and rapid experimentation will be rewarded with motivated teams and a productive organization.

\*   \*   \*

We have organized this book around three broad categories relevant to every general manager: managing the business, managing others and managing yourself.

The first section, Managing the Business, provides a concrete business context for the more personal leadership issues discussed in the latter two sections. The three chapters in Section 1 will examine the idea of long-term value creation, explore the implications of a long-term value perspective on business decisions and conclude with the importance of translating an understanding of the concept into actual financial calculations.

Section 2, Managing Others, deals with the difficult leadership transition of managing your team in a new context – that is, as a general rather than a functional manager. As the functional manager transitions to a role of general management, the challenge now becomes one of managing the managers, a greater challenge than was managing the doers who were often merely waiting to be told what to do. Good GMs do not simply tell the managers what to do; they seek ways to motivate, encourage and maintain a shared commitment toward the goal of value creation, without actually telling anyone what to do.

The key to success in managing others is the kind of communication that fosters an open environment perceived by all as fair and trusting. The three chapters in Section 2 deal with the new relationships created by the altered hierarchical positioning and the according need for improved communication, the challenge of managing different personal and political factors and, finally, the importance of both separating emotions from decision-making and keeping biases, personal agendas and opinions out of the process.

In the final section, Managing Yourself, we delve into the deep personal awareness needed to be a fully-performing general manager. At this stage of the journey, the only thing that matters is the ability to learn how to learn – constantly, and without allowing opinion, personal agendas or political manoeuvering to compromise value-based decision-making and effective management of those around you.

To become truly successful leaders, general managers must embrace their own individual journeys, which will in turn allow them to complete the transformation into ongoing creators of value for their organizations. The three chapters in this final section tackle three highly sensitive and important issues: managing one's own feelings in order to empathize with others while remaining an objective and effective leader, becoming comfortable and confident about one's role without having to be an expert on each topic or feeling a sense of competition among your peers and, finally, successfully managing subconscious motivations, to remain effective, fair and, as ever, value-oriented.

*   *   *

In the chapters that follow, you will encounter each GM's individual scenario via a description or transcript of the situation in which they find themselves, mirroring what we showed on the videos in the interactive platform. Also listed are the specific questions we asked our participants to respond to. We then proceed to a general discussion about the comments received from our contributors, according to specific themes that emerged and, finally, to our own commentary regarding the original situation, the varying factors at play, the reactions and behaviours of the particular GM, and what it means to his or her overall evolution.

Our goal in creating these general managers and their respective passages was not merely to solicit reactions from those already familiar with the ideas we teach. It was to highlight the multifaceted changes that anyone must face if he or she is to succeed as a GM in a truly global, rapidly changing and fiercely competitive world.

Allow us to introduce our three fictional GMs:

FREDDY

**Freddy Walsh** is VP IT, North America, for Prism International, a New York City-based media conglomerate focused on distribution of film and television content, with over 5000 employees and offices in 15 cities across the globe. Freddy has held four different positions within Prism over the course of a dozen years. He has moved three times during his tenure with the company, first from his native Toronto to San Francisco, then from San Francisco to the company's headquarters in New York City. This most recent move is just weeks old, and coincides with Freddy's promotion to the current position, which now makes him part of Prism's senior management team.

With the traditional revenue model collapsing and media going increasingly digital, Prism International is in decline, as evidenced by shrinking market share and decreased revenues. The need for a new strategy is overwhelmingly clear, but senior management is showing a collective reluctance to throw off the chains and take action. Freddy believes radical change is needed, but he lacks the communication, leadership and persuasion skills to get others on his side. He feels his logic is sound, but he's never been great at winning others over to his opinion. As an IT guy, his expertise is in logic and explanation, not rhetoric or debate. Freddy feels there is a need to experiment, learn quickly and adapt to the changing consumer and technological reality. But he struggles to express his opinion – plus, he's the new guy.

**Nancy Iwala**, a second-generation African American, is Senior Finance Advisor with The Tipton Group, a midsize steel manufacturer in Pittsburgh. Nancy joined Tipton after spending a decade in various finance positions at Whitesands, a regional sugar refinery and distributor. Whitesands was a highly-siloed company, where Nancy held a senior position but collaborated little with her counterparts in other divisions. Though she had considerable influence over Finance-related decisions, she rarely had to discuss or debate decisions with anyone outside her own department.

Tipton's previous CEO, Miguel Jimenez, left the company just before Nancy arrived, part of the fallout from an accounting scandal that shook the organization. The company has grown steadily for over a decade and, despite the sound business foundation that remains, is now in a precarious financial position, leading to a plummeting stock price and shareholder nervousness about what strategic direction the company will take. Nancy's role is one of half a dozen that have been replaced.

**Hugo van Groten** is a newly-promoted General Manager at AMR, a Brussels-based distributor of kids' toys. Hugo has been with AMR for 14 years. It is the only company he has ever worked for. Hugo came directly out of his MBA and into a marketing position, and has ascended the marketing ladder with AMR over the course of his career. He has been promoted to GM EMEA from his previous role as Director of Marketing. His new role makes him part of the dozen-strong executive team. He will now report to Daisuke 'Dino' Tai, AMR's CEO.

We hope that the concepts we discuss and the views we provide in this book will help you embark on the journey toward general management with confidence and clarity, and that you will form your own thinking around the issues and challenges we present via the journeys of Freddy, Nancy and Hugo. To that end, at the conclusion of each scenario discussion, we include a box called 'Your Thoughts'. We encourage you to pause, reflect on what you've watched and read, and record some of your own contemplations.

Everyone's context is different, and it is not accurate to say that one success formula applies to every individual in every situation. However, we do confidently assert that the concepts presented in this book, considered properly and applied diligently, will provide a foundation from which effective general management can result. In these pages, Freddy, Nancy and Hugo will tackle the most crucial aspects of becoming a successful GM in today's business arena, and they will undergo the essential changes in personal and professional mindset that can translate, ultimately, into ongoing success.

We wish the same for you.

# Section 1
# Managing the Business

# Chapter 1

---

# Embracing the Why

## Freddy

### The Scenario

*Freddy is in his office unpacking boxes, putting pictures of his family on his desk, etc. He hears an e-mail ding into his Inbox on his desktop computer. The e-mail, marked urgent, is from Trish McDougall, Head of Technology and Operations North America. The other half-dozen members of the New York management team are copied on the e-mail as well. Trish is requesting a meeting to discuss the need for a new strategy.*

*Part of the senior management team assembles. In addition to Freddy and Trish, present is Vivian Ho, SVP IT, North America, to whom Freddy reports. Absent are Gil Stanton, VP Operations NA, and Patrick White, SVP Operations NA, all of whom report to Trish as well.*

*Here's how their conversation goes:*

TRISH: It's no secret that things have been going downhill, and we need to turn the ship around. The CEO is asking for opinions from all sides, which he's then going to consider before deciding on a strategy.

VIVIAN: Trish, I think it's important not to panic. A conservative approach makes sense, and it should be done from a cost-cutting perspective. The immediate focus should be on doing whatever it takes to stop the bleeding.

FREDDY: Is there an appetite here for … serious change?

TRISH: How do you mean, Freddy?

FREDDY: Exploring new opportunities. Riding the digital wave.

TRISH: That takes time. The market expects results.

FREDDY: I wonder if the traditional diversification strategy is working in the new environment. We've always had our fingers in a lot of pies, and it has worked. But maybe now we're spread too thin.

VIVIAN: What are you suggesting?

FREDDY: Avoiding risk is obviously good, but maybe it also comes with a danger of, I guess, spinning our wheels. We're in a lot of segments where it doesn't seem like we have any future.

VIVIAN: Spinning our wheels?

FREDDY: I'd be worried about doing a version of the same thing, but doing more of it. The diversification strategy was put in place years ago, and it worked, but I don't think it really works now. There are competitors in specific segments with superior value propositions. We're losing market share because of it. With a new reality, I think maybe it calls for real innovation to succeed in the long term.

VIVIAN: What about the short term? We're hemorrhaging. Keeping the portfolio diverse is exactly what will allow us to withstand the short-term changes.

FREDDY: Of course. I mean, you need something for the short term and for the long term. I haven't thought it all the way through …

VIVIAN: It's dangerous to overhaul the strategy. Incremental change makes sense, but by turning everything on its ear, well … I think it would be perceived by the market as a knee-jerk reaction. Change is good, but it should be done slowly and thoughtfully.

TRISH: I agree. Survival is the primary goal right now.

FREDDY: I hear what you're saying … what you're both saying. I just, I heard someone say once, even if you cut off the bad branches and feed the good ones, if the trunk is diseased you really aren't changing anything. You know what I mean.

TRISH:      Not really.

FREDDY:   You're saying cut off the bad branches and feed the good ones, or whatever, but the trunk of the tree is still there.

TRISH:      Okay. We're going to let this percolate for a bit and then push the discussion forward. I'd like each of you to think on this further and then send me an e-mail outlining what you think is the best strategy, and why, by noon Friday. Thanks for your views. We're adjourned.

## Questions We Asked

1. Have you ever argued for or against a diversification strategy? What position did you take? How was it received?
2. Have you ever been in a discussion where you felt your colleagues or bosses were adopting a short-term view to the potential disadvantage of the company? Did you say anything?
3. Have you ever had a different view than your immediate supervisor on an important topic? Did you make your opinion known? How was it received and what was the outcome?

## Comments We Got

The user community provided numerous anecdotes describing sensitive situations they've encountered just like the one faced by Freddy – whether it was to argue for or against diversification, debate short-term wins versus long-term gain, or take on their boss when they thought he or she wasn't necessarily seeing things clearly. They reported extensively on the classic challenge that arises for many general managers stuck at the crossroads of authority. Often, the greatest requirement of a GM in this position is to be able to argue effectively, at the right times, for the right causes, in the right way.

Six overall themes emerged from the input we received. Here they are, including some of the representative comments made.

1. **It's okay to argue for change. Change means innovation, and innovation means value.**

   'You have to take a risk. Otherwise, sooner or later, you will be out of the competition.'

   'After the financial crisis, "long-term" suddenly became equal to a quarter. I spoke up.'

   'Short-term strategy is cost-saving, but this will not be sustainable in the long term. As a member of the supervisory board, I'm trying to help the managing director to shift her focus gradually.'

   'The phrase "The markets wants …" or "The market is expecting …" comes up often. But seriously – I think that the market is more concerned about a sound long-term business plan than some kind of EBITDA make-up.'

2. **Articulate your position with data.**

   'When arguing against diversification I relied on the lack of value in pursuing it – expected results from the new directions were smaller than in focusing existing resources on the current mission.'

   'My approach is to gather the facts on overall developments in the market, our share development over time versus competitors, present them in a format that will allow discussion, start the discussion and ask the team who is winning and why.'

   'If you're going to suggest going away from your current direction, you should bring insight, and a plan.'

   'Fact basis and risk analysis were the essence of making my opinion known.'

3. **Build trust early and often, so that your opinions will matter.**

   'I prefer to have one-to-one conversations to build my vision before positioning myself.'

'I have learned to choose my battles and argue against decisions only when there is a "material harm" for the company. In those cases, I choose to influence the course of action behind the scenes, not in meetings, and try to form coalitions or find common ground with other members of the management team.'

'In my experience, it is greatly appreciated when you speak up and give your opinion, but only when your relationship is developed in such a way that your supervisor trusts you.'

'I will work hard to support my boss. This will ensure I gain trust and respect, at least for hard work and loyalty. It will also ensure that he understands I support him and it's not my intention to undermine him or his authority. Once I gain that trust, only then will I be more open with my opinions.'

4. **Remove any personal agenda. Focus on value for the company.**

'I argued for a diversification strategy, and it was well received. Everyone agreed to move forward in a certain direction. Then the group divided themselves in reality. Some people spent their time slowing the process, while others strategically moved to ensure they would get what they believed they needed for their respective market or area of responsibility.'

'The approach that I take always comes from customers' needs, as that is the driver for all businesses.'

'Experts protect their own little corners.'

'I find bringing the discussion back to customer and shareholder value works, as does linking in with the customer values.'

'The internal personal decision that has to be made each time is: (i) take a stand and make a statement, (ii) I am keeping my mouth shut in order to survive and fight another day, or (iii) I don't care, as long as I get paid. The difference between the first two is often seniority and the number of people in the room.'

'Being right, and getting the individual credit, is not what matters. Successfully expressing an alternative, sometimes in steps, and getting others to start seeing it and then being willing to discuss it is how you can best contribute. For that, it is important to keep yourself out of the centre of attention.'

### 5. Know that people are going to resist change.

'Often I get a negative response, and frankly I think it is because senior officers are afraid of admitting a wrong strategy or fear the loss of prestige when leaving marketplaces where our competitors are well established and making profits.'

'I approached my supervisor and discussed the need for our company to engage in a diversification strategy, adding to our value proposition of supply of equipment for the Oil & Gas operators and contractors the business line of services in the Upstream and Downstream sectors, to weather off the cyclicality of trading and position the company on the Opex Spending Stream of our clients. My proposal was supported and raised to our Board, who turned it down when the underlying investment requirements were presented to them. I took the decision to leave, as I believed that I could not continue serving the same original vision. My boss followed suit a year or so later. In 2001, I was called back to rejoin the same company and the new established Board gave me the go-ahead to launch the same strategy presented to their predecessors three years earlier. The toughest part from thereon was gaining the minds of the colleagues to help build up a whole new organization. My ex-boss rejoined us a year later and we formed a team with distinct responsibilities, his was keeping the Board in line with the plan, and mine was developing the business, running the new operations launched, and getting the organization in harmony.'

'Even though the need for change may be there, it usually takes lots of meetings and conversations to open eyes, cross conservative mindsets, and achieve radical change. Keep explaining your idea. Keep your message alive. If it's worthwhile, eventually someone will pick it up and support you.'

'Cutting off the weak branches is a tough thing to do.'

'I am constantly amazed at the stranglehold that Wall Street and, many times, kids a couple of years out of school have on our ability to sacrifice short-term for long-term value growth.'

'Reactions are almost always 'I hear you but you don't understand the big picture' or similar.'

6. **Challenge in private, not publicly; don't undermine or 'take on' your boss; understand that even if you present your position well, it still may be rejected.**

'On topics where you know that a challenge to the decision is political suicide, and/or that the arguing against is a lost cause anyhow, then my argumentation might not be as firm.'

'Any discussion and/or challenging of an opinion will have to happen behind closed doors. When the doors open again, then it's "United we stand".'

'I did everything I could, including putting together a detailed report, inviting other people from other departments or external advisors, and using upper management influence. It sometimes worked, sometimes not.'

'Even when the decision is against your opinion, executive orders sometimes have to be taken.'

'We almost always find a mutual compromise. But when we don't, we follow his opinion.'

'There were two separate instances in which I tried to shift management views and was overruled. In the first, the potential consequences were not financial, so I let it go and accepted the team decision, then kept my mouth shut when things turned out exactly as I had predicted. In the second instance, once management had made the decision, I called and e-mailed various higher levels of management to try to intercept the decision (without being disloyal), since the consequences were more serious. The decision was unfortunately maintained and a massive cluster-f@&k ensued. (Un)fortunately there was no witch hunt to find those responsible. It's important to pick your battles, play by the rules and not hold a grudge when things go wrong.'

'It is okay to voice your opinion in one-to-one discussions. To take the dialogue in a meeting with a bigger audience has seldom turned out successful.'

## Our Thoughts

As the new guy on the block, Freddy finds himself immediately having to wrestle with a significant dilemma: does he argue for the long-term-value approach he sincerely believes in or kowtow to the more short-term strategies being endorsed by both his colleague Vivian and his boss Trish? Freddy can't and won't know the motivations of either one of them, but they seem to be driven strongly by short-term concerns about risk. Diversification strategies can sometimes be proposed and upheld by managers who are more concerned about their own short-term risk rather than the long-term health of the company.

If the industry is changing at a rapid pace and competition is starting to come from more focused competitors taking new approaches to specific aspects of their business, there is little hope that Prism International can continue to out-compete these new competitors across a diversified portfolio. Prism must examine where its strengths lie, and focus on re-shaping its business. But Vivian and Trish's risk-aversion is driving them to seek shelter in what they see as short-term safety.

This is a classic trade-off general managers must learn to make: *How can I separate my own short-term interests in keeping a diversified portfolio, which might help to mitigate risks in the short term, with the long-term interests of the company to develop sustainable competitive advantage, which might require actions that increase short-term risk?* Freddy is now caught in the middle of this debate. As the new guy in the organization, he sees the need for change to drive its long-term health while the existing team prefers to seek short-term safety in a diversification strategy they feel has worked in the past.

Freddy needs to balance his belief in what is good for the long-term health of the company with the freshness of his managerial status. He can't go in with guns blazing, demanding that everyone see it his way. He has neither the seniority nor the credibility for this, and in any event Vivian and Trish both seem fairly set in 'safe' mode for now: cut costs, show the market what it wants to see, seek shelter amid the storm. Freddy's 'Why' is being tested in his first days on the job. He must ask himself just how much he believes in the long-term value perspective he is so desperately trying to convey to Vivian and Trish.

Freddy seems to recognize that he can only push so hard, but it is clear that he feels strongly about the direction Prism needs to take if it is to survive in the long term. There is no such thing as not taking a risk here. Rolling over carries with it the risk of losing his job should the company collapse amid what he sees as an ill-fated strategy; arguing his point too aggressively carries the same risk, for different reasons. So where does that leave Freddy, who is obviously struggling to make himself heard against the tandem stonewall of Vivian and Trish?

We suggest Freddy stay resolute in his thinking but start to develop a more substantial, more concrete argument. As someone accustomed to talking in IT language, it will help him to bring structure and data to the discussion, rhetoric clearly not being a strong suit of his. Though Vivian appears pretty narrow-minded about the topic, it is Trish who is Freddy's boss, and she seems open enough to continued discussion. At a minimum, she is offering him a second chance at presenting the argument that she recognizes he is trying to verbalize, even if she doesn't quite know what that argument is yet because of Freddy's lack of ability to express himself clearly. He should seize the opportunity Trish is giving him. Change is seldom accomplished without someone sticking their neck out for something they believe in.

**Your Thoughts**

# Nancy

## The Scenario

*A meeting is called by the new CFO, Calvin Lee, to whom Nancy now reports. Cal is the interim acting CEO while the board seeks a replacement. Also present is Nancy's colleague Dana Klein, SVP Finance, who reports to Calvin as well. Dana has been with Tipton for six years and survived the scandal. The subject line in the meeting invite was 'Discuss new direction'.*

*When Nancy walks into Calvin's office, Dana is already there. Here's how the conversation proceeds:*

CALVIN:   Okay. The shareholders are getting nervous, and the board has asked that we provide a recommendation on how to proceed.

NANCY:   I think we need to develop a new strategy with specific targets on key performance indicators, which we can then communicate to the markets. Specific timelines, delivery promises, names and incentives attached to each target. It will re-establish our credibility. It will also let the staff know how their performance is measured.

DANA:   I respectfully disagree. If we're going to reposition the business, we can't do it according to the same strategy that landed us here. Miguel may have been charismatic with the media, but he was also reckless. Targets matter, but they shouldn't be the focus.

NANCY:   I don't understand what you're disagreeing with.

DANA:   Miguel felt KPIs were the be-all and end-all. But by defining strategy as a series of targets on KPIs, and then driving the management team to hit those targets, he's put us in a precarious situation. What we need now is a strategy that isn't dumbed down to a series of targets, but rather is about rebuilding the company.

NANCY:   My suggestion isn't to set arbitrary targets and then see what happens. It's to get smarter about how targets are set, so the staff will be better motivated to hit them.

DANA:   Targets are used to help us learn about whether we're delivering, but strategy and management should be more nuanced than that. Just motivating staff to hit targets is what got us into the current mess. Pursuing the same approach is going to look bad to shareholders.

CALVIN:   Let's leave the shareholders out of it for a moment and focus on what we think is the best direction for the company.

NANCY:    I think targets impose structure, and they give people something tangible to aim for.

DANA:     Miguel was all about conventional wisdom – target-based compensation, balanced scorecards, etc. I know that's been the trend, but we need to think about long-term value, which is different than hitting targets. KPIs represent short-term thinking if they aren't part of a broader approach.

NANCY:    I'm unclear what you mean by the difference between hitting targets and creating value. If we set targets and hit them, how are we not creating value?

DANA:     Getting people to hit targets may increase productivity, at least on the surface. But that doesn't necessarily mean we're moving in the right direction. If you hit your goals better, but they're the wrong goals, it doesn't move you forward, it moves you back.

NANCY:    But how can you expect people to hit long-term targets if you don't give them short-term targets? How will we motivate people to take the right kind of action?

CALVIN:   Okay – I appreciate both your views, and I'd like you to think more about them. We're going to reconvene tomorrow and continue the discussion. We need to present to the board in a week. Thanks.

## Questions We Asked

1. Have you ever been in a discussion about a shift in company strategy following a crisis? What was your role in it? Did you generally agree with the views of others, or did you offer a contrasting view? What path did the company take?
2. Have you ever been in a debate about hitting short-term targets versus creating long-term value? What was your view and how was it received?
3. Does your organization use KPIs? How? Do you find it effective?

## Comments We Got

Nancy's mildly heated discussion with Dana in Calvin's office elicited lots of passionate responses. People clearly feel strongly about the short-term versus long-term debate – as they should – and they feel equally strongly about the responsibility of general managers to push for the right kinds of value-driven goals while remaining politically strategic. (One of our respondents even managed to use the word 'incentivize'. Nice.)

We were fascinated by the things our participants had to say about the often tricky world general managers must navigate. They shared with us a multitude of experiences that point to the new demands placed on GMs as they assume their new positions – demands that come in various forms and from numerous sources. Here are the five major themes reflected in our participants' input, with representative comments.

**1. It isn't easy for GMs to find their place as change agents.**

'To effectively drive changes and implement new strategy, it is important that general managers have the opportunity to regularly review the progress of change/transformation with those setting the strategy so that we can confirm our impact and contribution. We can sometimes be "lost in translation".'

'My contributions have been mostly to connect these dots to the lower levels in the organization: as long as people see the strategic long-term direction and understand how their KPIs and short-term targets relate to the bigger picture, it works. As a leader you need to express confidence and help shape programmes while defending them to the people reporting to you.'

**2. Short-terms goals should be building blocks toward long-term value.**

'GMs should at all times understand how their day-to-day/short-term activities, and those of their teams, contribute to long-term value. GMs must go beyond the idea that "short term compromises long term" and have a duty to make sure that whatever they do, they "build now for the long term" – the real meaning of sustainability at large. I consider it a duty of general managers to orchestrate short-term actions without compromising long-term value. To fulfil this duty, they must be clear about the value chain and the contribution of themselves and their teams.'

'Management has to be able to explain that short-term targets are aligned to a greater vision. Most companies don't do a good job of explaining how short-term targets fit into a larger mission.'

'In crisis mode, short-term measures are used to get the profits right. Unfortunately, this can lead to brain drain if people don't understand the future picture.'

'Discussions about short-term strategy usually happen close to year-end when targets have not been met. What is important is to understand the implications that short-term knee-jerk reactions could have on the long-term strategy.'

'Short-term targets are needed, even to reach long-term goals, because it gives people a means to focus and to gain successes.'

'My view remains that, although our focus should be on creating long-term value, there must be short-term steps or actions to take to achieve this, and they must be measured. We mustn't focus so much on short-term targets to the detriment of creating long-term value.'

'My view is to always be focused on building long-term value, but there needs to be the right measures in place to incentivize the right short-term behaviour.'

### 3. It isn't easy to figure out KPIs.

'My company used KPIs. I found them totally counterproductive and I tried to insist that we stop using such metrics, or use them differently.'

'We use KPIs. This is partly effective, because it facilitates discussion about performance. They are not used for bonuses.

We're still struggling to determine and calculate meaningful KPIs.'

'We have a lot of KPIs – too many. I agree that KPIs are essential to understand the business, but not necessarily to drive the business. A company needs to deliver value to the shareholder or owner on a long-term basis. That is the only KPI that matters at the end of the day.'

'KPIs are not relevant for the vast part of the organization, starting with middle management and employees without managerial responsibilities. The further out in the organization the employee, the less relevant the KPIs.'

'KPIs are essential to measure the true effectiveness of an organization. However, too many indicators don't tell you if you are going to hit a roadblock or run out of gas soon. KPIs are efficient if they are aligned with a list of defined objectives for the company and they remain coherent from the executive team to those in the field.'

'We moved away from KPIs in measuring performance, as we realized in time that, no matter how smart they are, KPIs can and will be managed. However, at project levels and down to the smallest measurable tasks, we use them intensively as they create a good sense of achievement if they are simple, clear and visible to those delivering them.'

## 4. GMs are expected to speak their minds, but also toe the line.

'I find large organizations quite ambivalent toward change agents at the GM level. They encourage constructive and inclusive contribution but expect them, as GMs, to support a certain managerial rhetoric. Not an easy place to be.'

'I am always advocating for long-term value, but being part of a larger corporation, we end up doing the silly short-term things. Fortunately, we have found ways to satisfy the short-term KPIs while doing long-term work. Life would be easier, and more value would be generated, from not having to do the short-term things.'

'Keeping people focused on long-term goals takes a sustained effort.'

'I kept focused on the long-term strategy and avoided debates on short-term risks and rewards. This demanded a lot of resilience and continuous communication on the long-term benefits and identification of indicators that are tangible enough for the short-term fans to relate to in order to keep the momentum for the long term.'

'My view was that we must keep our focus on creating long-term value for the purpose of sustaining our business, and at the same time put short-term targets in measurable terms.'

5. **People will push short-term goals for all sorts of reasons – usually personal ones.**

'It is very complicated to sacrifice short-term advantages for long-term sustainability. The structure and framework have to be very clear to prevent individuals focusing on their own interests, which are generally short-term oriented.'

'Short-term goals are effective to some extent if the target is clear and people work toward the goal. However, it is seldom easy to detect if such effort is just for the short term, even if destroying long-term value.'

'Short-term targets tend to have a wrong feeling to them, even when their negative impact cannot be easily pinpointed. I am almost always against them.'

'It's almost always an uphill battle to get people focused on long-term value and to get them to work harder at the same time.'

'I was a team leader of a declining business and had to deal with a group of newcomers who wanted to change everything. It seemed to me they wanted to change just for the sake of change. A newly proposed strategy was in essence not different from the one we had already. Based on their recommendations, we let some experienced people go. But the business did not turn around.'

## Our Thoughts

Nancy is facing a somewhat similar quandary to that encountered by Freddy: in her first days on the job, she finds herself unexpectedly going up against a colleague whose views seem to diverge violently from her own on a matter of grave importance. The matter in this case is the use of Key Performance Indicators and their potential impact on driving short-term results versus long-term value. Nancy's colleague Dana is arguing that the company should be using KPIs somehow differently, but Nancy is getting frustrated by what seems to her as empty words – she doesn't really understand what Dana is trying to say. As far as Nancy is concerned, KPIs give people structure and goals and therefore motivation, and what does a company want if not motivated staff?

The argument that Nancy must now face is even more subtle and challenging than the one in which Freddy found himself. Nancy is not arguing for a short-term perspective, only for the use of KPIs to drive behaviours. Dana is trying to express her objection to KPIs by linking them to behaviours focused only on short-term results. The argument is difficult to express and thus lost on Nancy. Nancy's resulting frustration is in response to what appear to be hollow words on the part of her new colleague.

Interestingly, the comments we received highlighted both Nancy's and Dana's viewpoints, while also converging into a single general view that KPIs and short-term targets *can* be used effectively, but are almost always *not* used effectively. We agree. In our observation, short-term targets are used naively in the best of cases and hazardously in the worst of them. KPIs and similar metrics can reveal a great deal about what your company does, how it functions and what it can do better, but only if they are used as a window into your operations and not as an objective unto themselves. This is what Dana is trying to communicate to Nancy and Calvin, but she is doing a poor job of it.

As a result, Nancy is bristling, and digging in her own heels. She probably doesn't even recognize how defensively she is behaving, though the tension between her and Dana escalates quickly and is certainly recognized by Calvin. In our view, Nancy needs to take a step back and think hard about her new position and what it means in the context of her new firm. In her previous role at White-sands, the sugar refinery, she had considerable authority within her highly-siloed department, but little interaction outside of it, therefore she probably didn't have to think much beyond the targets and objectives set within her own confined world.

The Tipton Group, a steel manufacturer, has a different organizational structure, one that emphasizes collaboration and joint decision-making. Nancy's role and responsibilities will now require her to think much more broadly across various aspects of the business, making simple KPIs difficult to implement effectively and consistently across departments and reasonable time horizons. Nancy was so accustomed to her old, more functional environment that Dana's argument, even if less than clear, is now a shock to Nancy's system, causing her instinctively to rebel. This kind of reaction will not serve her well in her new managerial role at Tipton.

**Your Thoughts**

## Hugo

### The Scenario

*Yesterday, Hugo walked into the main boardroom, where the executive team was gathered for their monthly meeting. Taking a moment to remind himself that he, too, is now a member of this senior group, he took a seat beside Dino, trying to act normal, though admittedly he was nervous. He reminded himself to just stick with what he knew. He watched as the video link to the Chicago office was uploaded and greetings were exchanged by the two Senior Vice Presidents heading the meeting. Hugo had reviewed the agenda distributed two days before, which focused on an important new investment decision for AMR.*

*At a critical point in the meeting, Hugo was asked his opinion about the investment decision. Hugo offered Marketing's perspective on the investment, then listened to the views given by others around the table. As he listened to the emerging conversation, he realized that most of the opinions being shared ran counter to his, and he began to feel vulnerable and lacking in knowledge. He left the meeting feeling his contribution had been roundly viewed as unimpressive, even though nobody said so.*

*Following the meeting, Dino asked Hugo to come to his office for a chat. Here is the exchange that followed:*

DINO:     Hi, Hugo. Have a seat. How did you think the meeting went this morning?

HUGO:     I enjoyed it. I'm happy to be part of the executive team.

DINO:     And the team is happy you're part of it. But I think you might have felt a little uncomfortable today. Is that accurate?

HUGO:     Yes. I felt my opinion of the investment opportunity was in the minority.

DINO:     It was. Listen, I want to help you understand something. I was Marketing Director before you and then, like you, GM EMEA. My first meeting with the executive team was similar. There was a

|  | |
|---|---|
|  | new investment tabled – we were considering acquiring a small toy company out of London. The partners wanted to know what everyone thought about it. I gave what I thought was a sound view, but when everyone else spoke it was like they were contradicting what I'd said. Kind of like you probably felt today. |
| HUGO: | Yes. |
| DINO: | The reason was that I talked to the opportunity from Marketing's perspective, which was what I knew best. But your new business card doesn't say Marketing Director anymore. |
| HUGO: | I don't understand. |
| DINO: | You walked in there thinking, my job is to demonstrate my marketing expertise. That's why I was promoted to this role after all. Right? |
| HUGO: | Well … |
| DINO: | It's natural. You've spent years learning how to be a great marketer. That's why you've continued to rise. But here's the irony: You need to forget all that. |
| HUGO: | What do you mean? |
| DINO: | When you're sitting around the executive table, you can't think from the perspective of marketing exclusively. Nobody cares what that potential investment means to any one division. They care what it means to the company. |
| HUGO: | But marketing is my area of expertise. How am I supposed to not speak from a marketing perspective? |
| DINO: | Everyone in that room was a functional expert in something first. But now you have to think of yourself as a member of the group making company-wide decisions. |
| HUGO: | It sounds like you're telling me to forget everything I've learned. |
| DINO: | Bingo! You've been taught to do one thing very well. That's what the company needed from you – until now. Starting today, it needs you to start thinking more broadly. |
| HUGO: | How can I think more broadly if my training is in one area? |
| DINO: | No one expects you to become an across-the-board expert overnight. But you will have to start building knowledge in other disciplines to optimize your contribution. I'm talking about both perspective and competence. |

HUGO: You mean I'm expected to become an IT expert? An operations expert? A finance– ?

DINO: Not quite. You're expected to make every decision from a perspective of creating value for the company. You're no longer a functional expert. You're a facilitator of value for the company. Get it?

HUGO: I think so.

DINO: Feeling a bit overwhelmed?

HUGO: Yes.

DINO: Welcome aboard.

## Questions We Asked

1. Have you ever been told that you needed to change your perspective in order to become a more effective contributor? What part of this process did you find most challenging? What were the key success factors to your change in perspective (when you were successful)?
2. Have you ever been asked to broaden your range of knowledge or expertise in order to become a more effective leader? Who suggested it, what did they suggest, and what did you do in response?
3. Have you ever been asked to think beyond your own area of functional expertise? How difficult a challenge was it and what were the benefits to you and the organization?

## Comments We Got

Many people shared experiences in which it was necessary for them, for one reason or another, to step outside of where they'd been. Whether in terms of role, function or expertise, if there's one part of being a general manager that seems to have resonated most commonly with our participants, it is the necessity to break out of one's previous mould. This can mean many different things, from acquiring new knowledge to learning new methods to assuming new perspectives. And, as different members of the group told us in different ways, none of it is easy. Here are the themes that came through from our participants' thoughts, including some illustrative comments.

1. **Force yourself outside your comfort zone. Leave what you know behind.**

   'Transitioning to general management means that you have to unburden yourself from your functional past.'

   'I just started letting go of things.'

2. **Listen to, and learn from, others.**

   'Do a lot of listening, looking and learning.'

   'Listen and listen again to others. Above, under and around me.'

   'Key success factor for me to change was to always ask feedback from my team before an important exec meeting. Their views allowed me to elevate my thinking.'

   'What I try to do is listen carefully to what the experts in each area say and think. The story I never accept is, "This is the way it has been done in the past".'

   'If you are asked to think beyond your area, start learning the language of that area and develop relationships with people who can help you in those areas (Network). My current projects are with Finance as well as Legal. For Legal, I'm taking three attorneys I work with out for drinks every two months just to chat.'

3. **Think delegation/empowerment over control/micromanagement.**

   'Build complementary teams and let the team come to the right conclusions – make them responsible for the execution in a way that they believe in.'

   'At first, I tried to be an expert in all fields. That did not work. I then made the functional experts accountable for their work, but also for informing me and sometimes even educating me. That worked better.'

   'This is important, because it gives the new manager the space he needs to explore his way of working.'

   'I feel the business is benefitting from me being a more efficient cross-functional manager. It is helped by having a functional lead reporting to me who is very effective and allowed me to leave him to do his business with little involvement from me.'

4. **Think about asking the right questions instead of offering solutions.**

'Before, I always thought asking questions makes me vulnerable. The opposite is the case.'

5. **Figure out how to distance yourself from being a 'consultant' in your former function.**

'Due to my expertise in a certain area, I am still consulted frequently and have a tendency to get involved.'

6. **Recognize that it's an ongoing effort.**

'It remains a constant challenge, especially as I retain some of the technical functions of my last assignment.'

'Each day I have to think beyond my own expertise.'

## Our Thoughts

Hugo is going through the most obvious, but also the most difficult, aspect of the transition from functional to general management. Functional experts are taught to see things from a narrow perspective and encouraged to do one thing very well. Marketing managers, IT leads, operations heads – all are groomed to develop expertise along one track, often with their heads down and blinders on. Once tapped to become general managers, these functional experts know only to bring that same narrow perspective to the executive table.

Unfortunately, this is a recipe for disaster, and Dino is trying to send that message to Hugo from the start, as clearly as he can. He is telling Hugo that successful GMs must abandon everything they know in deference to the bigger goal of making decisions that create organizational value. Hugo must understand that he is moving from the role of functional expert to facilitator of value. Only then can he be ready to absorb, and put into action, the specific principles that all successful managers live by every day.

Hugo is clearly having difficulty understanding this message at even a basic level. He seems willing to learn, but perplexed and intimidated by what Dino is telling him.

We see this as a positive.

Why? Because Hugo, while he may not be clear about *how* to execute his new role, seems clear about learning *why* he needs to start to see himself in a new way. While he isn't quite lucid on the messages Dino is giving him, by the same token he is not demonstrating any resistance to them, and that willingness alone gives him an immediate leg up. If being a new GM is about anything, it is about displaying the flexibility and openness to shed one's previous skin and step into something totally new. Trying to apply the functional knowledge you used so well in your last role to this one will not work because, as Dino eloquently puts it, you are no longer a functional expert, but rather a facilitator of value, and your job now is to make, and encourage, decisions that create long-term value for the company. As many of our contributors pointed out, Hugo has a lot to learn about how to distance himself from his previous role, adopt a value-based perspective and take a long-term view. But at least he recognizes this need, which is the right place to start.

**Your Thoughts**

*  *  *

## Overall Discussion

As Freddy, Nancy and Hugo begin the transition from functional to general manager, each of them is embarking on a complex journey full of excitement and opportunity, but fraught with potential pitfalls. Some of these pitfalls they find right in front of them, before they have even had time to settle into their new role. Freddy is dealing with both a peer and boss who seem to be seeking safety in a strategy they hope will reduce short-term uncertainty, and thus are highly reluctant to change or innovate. Nancy is at odds with a colleague who aggressively rejects her ideas about short-term targets, confusing and unnerving her. Hugo has been jarred out of his previous comfort zone and is being asked to let go of what made him successful to this point in order to take on an entirely different role.

In facing this moment, our GMs have begun a multilayered process that is essential to their understanding of the place and the position they now occupy. They are breaking away from one group to join another; progressing from a role of specificity to one of aggregation; and adopting a new position for which they have no experience or prior knowledge, and therefore no reason to succeed. Those around them, both subtly and explicitly, are telling them that to thrive in this task they must first adopt a new way of thinking, and that to adopt a new way of thinking they must understand why it is necessary to do so.

The 'why' that they must embrace is the value perspective. Freddy must be able to argue the long-term health of the company to his boss and colleague, who are currently seeking refuge in what they see as the short-term safety of the firm's traditional diversification strategy. Nancy must find a way to fully appreciate what her colleague is trying to explain to her about the tendency of KPIs to drive short-term behaviours at the expense of long-term value creation. Hugo must be able to let go of the 'marketing perspective' and embrace the larger perspective of long-term organizational value. As is typical of new general managers, not one of the three came in prepared for this.

Critical to their success will be their active engagement in the change process, and their active rejection of any stubbornness or resistance driven by fear, hubris or bias. To adopt a value perspective is to embrace the long-term health of the company, to let go of one's natural tendency towards a functional view and to embrace a wider, organizational view. As Freddy, Nancy and Hugo are clearly illustrating, the journey into the uncharted territory of this new broader perspective often begins with frustration, confusion and anxiety.

## Key Questions to Ask Yourself

1. Are you consciously seeking to expand your vision and perspective to that of an organization-wide and long-term view?
2. Are you recognizing the changing perception of you and the changing expectations for your contribution?
3. Are you actively seeking input and creating 'experiments' to help you to learn and navigate this new journey into unfamiliar territory?

# Chapter 2

# Seeing the Implications

## Freddy

### The Scenario

*In his previous meeting with Trish and Vivian, Freddy tentatively argued for the need for innovation and long-term value creation, even in the face of potentially higher risk. Both Trish and Vivian, on the other hand, seemed to endorse a conservative approach, for reasons that at the moment remain a mystery to Freddy. Now, he is one of a group of people who receives an e-mail from senior management letting them know about a decision to be made that calls the very issue of value creation into question. Freddy knocks on Trish's door. Here's what transpires:*

FREDDY: Got a minute?

TRISH: Come on in.

FREDDY: I wanted to talk to you about the e-mail you sent to the management team.

TRISH: About the potential acquisition?

FREDDY: Yes.

TRISH: It's a small media company in the Midwest. Came straight from the managing directors' team.

FREDDY: Are you for it?

TRISH: I'm cautiously optimistic, though I haven't run any numbers yet. As we discussed, it's important to minimize risk, and diversification is one way to do that.

FREDDY:  What about the long-term value?

TRISH:  Long-term value is nice, but if we don't right this ship, we may not be around long enough to talk about it.

FREDDY:  I was wondering if we could book some time for you to take me through the typical analyses that the company performs when considering a move like this.

TRISH:  Typical analyses?

FREDDY:  I mean, what criteria are used, and according to what horizon, and who does the analysis? Is it just numbers-based, or is there more to it?

TRISH:  Yes, numbers have a lot to do with it. I guess it depends whose numbers you're referring to.

FREDDY:  That's exactly what I mean. Do you feel the numbers that are looked at are the right ones?

TRISH:  The right ones?

FREDDY:  I wish I could explain it better. It isn't my forte. I've been here for a dozen years, Trish. I've seen the company do some things I didn't always agree with, or not do some things I think it should have. Because we're in such a precarious position now, I have a concern about them going down that road again.

TRISH:  Fair enough. What do you propose we do about it?

FREDDY:  I guess I'm just encouraging us to take what I would say is a proper look at the potential decision. I'm not against spending, but this would be one hell of a bad time to spend unwisely.

TRISH:  Freddy, I hear what you're saying. At least I hear what I think you're trying to say. But to say it and have people hear it, you're going to need to figure out a way to articulate it better.

FREDDY:  I know.

TRISH:  Here's my suggestion. Take a look at the e-mail I sent, which provides some basic data. Don't give me an opinion on it. E-mail me back asking as many follow-up questions as you'd like. Ask me for more numbers, other angles to consider. I'm asking this for two reasons.

FREDDY:  What are they?

TRISH:  First, maybe if I force you to think about the other information you'd want, it will help you not only form an opinion on it, but also help explain your reasoning. Second, it will help to have those questions recorded so that, if I agree with you and we want to take that thinking to the directors, they'll know how we got there.

FREDDY:   Thanks, Trish.

TRISH:      Thank you.

FREDDY:   For what?

TRISH:      For speaking up.

## Questions We Asked

1. Have you ever felt a decision was being driven for non-value-based reasons, but you were unable to confront those proposing the idea? In retrospect, what might have made you more comfortable to speak up?
2. When alternative methods of 'analysis' are proposed to address the same question, what would be your suggestion, based upon your experience, for how to select the right alternative?
3. In your experience, when concerns other than 'the numbers' are being expressed to support a decision, how does one validate or invalidate these other concerns?

## Comments We Got

Collectively, the group of participants made numerous strong statements not only about the importance of seeking value-based decisions but also about the various roadblocks managers can face when trying to do so, including obstacles set up by those with greater seniority, bogus arguments that gain traction and support because of the level at which they are initiated, and an organizational culture that may not encourage – or, in some cases actively *dis*courage – constructive dissent.

Most members of the group also stressed the significance of a broad-based definition of value, one that involves more than just raw dollars seen on the surface of basic or traditional calculations. People seemed to agree that value isn't easy to measure, and it is something to be worked hard at, with arguments both for and against a given investment requiring proper justification. Participants had a lot of things to say about this topic, but they passionately agreed on one thing in general. The value impact of a given decision is often bigger than you think, and is generally not observable for some time; therefore it deserves more consideration than is typically given.

The overall remarks received centred around five broad themes. Here they are, along with a number of the more descriptive comments.

1. **Decisions driven from the top aren't always the right decisions.**

   'Our company had a very good market share at one customer in a low-end market, but not enough to make us profitable. Something had to change. The new CEO decided to reposition the company in the high end to get higher margins. This decision was non-value-based in a sense that (a) we could not bring enough value to the market in this segment and (b) the new CEO tried to repeat what he'd done at his previous company. Nobody could speak up, as he wasn't open to hearing any counter-opinions. People would have been more comfortable speaking up if an independent strategy group had looked at alternatives, rather than the CEO himself. After two years he was ousted and the company went belly-up.'

   'After completing an acquisition and divesting it two years later with a big return, I was asked to join a team led by my supervisor tasked with conducting a similar operation, with a view to short-to-medium-term divestment. The target acquisition is far from having the same criteria as the earlier one, and it is going to be very hard to create the value in it before considerable time has passed; I have to date been convinced that this is going to end up less positive than expected. I have been less vocal than I am used to being, as I felt my opinion would not matter and the excitement shown by the board and my supervisor – and the support I received from them – made me feel compelled to support their view. If I'd been engaged earlier and asked about the opportunity before the decision to acquire was taken, I would have argued against it.'

'Value driving was invoked for acquisitions or for portfolio rationalization in my company. While the numbers looked great for acquisitions, operationalizing the changes needed well-thought-through change management – which unfortunately did not happen, leading to chaos. In the case of product rationalization, management swung left and right on where to go in terms of whether to prioritize global versus local. An external consulting team would have helped get to the right place of value in both instances. I don't think I had the power to push for the solution.'

'I've seen non-value-based decisions in my organization loads of times. Some vague idea of value is presented with an unclear rationale behind it. Fair process would have helped to raise some questions. Instead, we all knew the guys in charge didn't like to be challenged.'

'In plenty of instances, ego plays a part. It's a fine line to question a superior, so facts are important, as is internal lobbying to gain support.'

'I've seen ideas and strategies that worked in other industries being applied – and failing – in a new company. Often it came down to the CEO/CFO taking the decisions without opening dialogue to others who might see it differently.'

## 2. Value-based decisions need to be articulated and justified.

'Working in a highly political, multi-stakeholder environment, a lot of decisions I have to deal with seem non-value-based. But I've learned to try to understand the value system of others. A fair-process environment would work best. You have to explain why each decision has been made.'

'I try to recommend value decisions based on solid business cases and a standard framework. My challenge is often to convince others, as internal company politics sometimes override sound business logic. I've learned to appoint a multi-functional inter-company team early in the process, to engage them in open and constructive discussions, and to establish shared assumptions and valuation models. It can also help to hire an external, independent firm to support the valuations.'

'Understanding the problem or question well and picking up the hidden details in it often gives the simplest answer or analysis of the situation.'

'There can be 100 prices, but there can only be one value. If we don't use the right process to find that number, additional computations won't help.'

'It's important to have a team work on a number of options and present to those with the right level of experience to make a final decision. You won't get it right 100% of the time, but not making a decision is worse.'

'The numbers are always wrong, but they should represent our best thinking and estimates, free of assumptions, and therefore provide a basis for value-based decisions.'

'Each time criteria other than data have been used to justify a decision, the deal has ended up in disaster, and the company has lost money. In each case, charismatic people have tried to persuade me, (ab)using their authority. At the end of the day, if you can't translate something into numbers, it's worth nothing.'

**3. Value involves multiple factors – don't ignore the less obvious ones.**

'Examine how each element impacts the decision. Let's say the new company is thought to have a significantly different culture than ours. This probably means it's going to be a long time before synergy savings are able to be captured. Also, if we are expecting the smaller company to inject an innovative culture and generate returns on new products, we should consider lengthening the time it's going to take to realize these returns. Each of these concerns will have some kind of financial impact that can be modelled and incorporated into the analysis.'

'In general, if the numbers look good, other factors, such as human factors, should be looked at as potentially impacting business value, sometimes as much as the raw numbers. Is the culture identical? Are people able to understand each other's businesses and work together?'

'Financial figures should not be the only parameters taken into account. Organizational and cultural aspects need to be addressed through systematic analysis as well.'

'You need to seek to capture non-numerical elements of the decision in numerical form. Whatever those concerns, if they cannot be defended or interpreted in numbers, it is left to judgement based on opinion or human factors only, which is dangerous.'

## 4. Counter-arguments need to be articulated and justified, too.

'I have seen decisions driven by non-value-based reasoning, presented with fake value propositions. But to make a counter-argument, I needed knowledge and experience in the subject that I didn't have. You need to offer a complete alternative instead of just questioning the one in front of you. That is often difficult.'

'In my experience, most decisions are made based on, in order, personal ambitions and beliefs, followed by the interests of the company. So decisions are heavily skewed by the benefits to the decision-maker. Therefore it can be tricky to challenge a hidden agenda. You need to uncover their real motivation.'

## 5. The company culture should encourage the asking of questions.

'I was a bit chicken to ask questions. I felt that just asking a question like "Can you help me understand the rationale behind this?" would get me in trouble. A sign of a sick company, I guess.'

'We recently attended a five-year planning session. During a management meeting, the CEO presented the reach goal numbers. No one believed them, but nobody spoke up either. To doubt the reach goal would have been seen as not being on board. We of course failed completely.'

## Our Thoughts

Freddy found out during the previous conversation that Vivian was risk-averse and Trish short-term oriented. It put him on the defensive right away, and he struggled to assert his point about the importance of innovation and seeking ways to create new value, even if it may run counter to what has been done before. Now, he and his peers have received word from Trish that the team of managing directors may be pursuing an opportunistic acquisition, and he has decided to be bold enough to ask her about the rationale behind the decision.

Trish tells Freddy she is 'cautiously optimistic', which, based on her conservative stance, may simply be a way of saying, 'I'm not going to question it'. Freddy seems to sense this instinctively, and perhaps fears that the proposed move is based on weak logic. He seems to understand a couple of important concepts. First, he understands that the company is in a precarious position and needs to show its stakeholders that it has a sound, thoughtful, long-term strategy to succeed in a changing arena. He also seems to understand that the company's shareholders are unlikely to be fooled by big moves made under false pretenses.

Already, Prism's share price is falling as its shareholders wait nervously to see what direction the company will take. Freddy intuitively grasps that action fuelled by short-term thinking is likely to make them even more skittish. His problem is that he has a difficult time explaining why this is. He has an almost visceral understanding of the need for a long-term perspective, and the fact that markets, despite their short-term reactiveness, also seek long-term return. His challenge now is to be able to articulate the implications of this perspective on a particular investment decision. All he can do is ask Trish whether she feels the numbers that the acquisition is being based on are 'the right ones'. It's a vague question, and therefore one that is basically impossible for Trish to answer.

Trish, to her credit, does two things right. First, she offers Freddy a little bit of room to challenge the logic behind the proposed acquisition. Second, she tells him at the same time that if he is going to question a senior management decision, he had better do so with a solid argument to back him up. 'I hear what you're saying,' she says. 'At least I hear what I think you're *trying* to say. But to say it and have people hear it, you're going to need to figure out a way to articulate it better.' She asks him to take a harder look at her initial e-mail and ask further, more pointed questions. She appears to agree with him that the implications for making a bad decision could be big, and she is allowing him to challenge senior executives regarding the decision, but only if he can present his argument the right way. This is a message Freddy needs to internalize if he is to succeed as a GM.

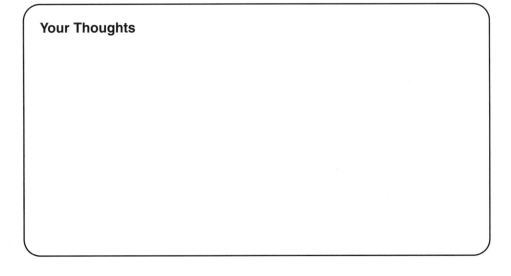

**Your Thoughts**

# Nancy

## The Scenario

*In her previous, somewhat tense meeting with Calvin Lee, CFO and acting CEO, and her colleague Dana Klein, SVP Finance, who also reports to Calvin, Nancy argued strenuously for a focus on hitting short-term targets and meeting KPIs. Her line of thinking was rejected directly by Dana, who felt that a broader, smarter strategy was necessary, in which indicators are only signs of deeper value drivers. Calvin himself remained mostly detached, encouraging both Nancy and Dana to think further on the topic.*

*Now, Nancy receives an e-mail from Calvin asking her back to his office for a follow-up discussion. Here's how the dialogue goes:*

CALVIN:   I wanted to talk to you a little more about that discussion we had earlier in the week. Dana has some pretty strong views, so I thought it might put you more at ease if you and I spoke one on one. I want you to know that I don't disagree with your statement that targets and KPIs can be highly valuable. I just want to make sure we look at them in the right context.

NANCY:   How do you mean?

CALVIN:   Well, I think it's kind of convenient to get caught up in the exercise of setting targets for people to hit and then, if they hit them, we say we're doing a good job. What would you say it's telling us?

NANCY:   I would say that if people are hitting the targets set for them, we are using our resources efficiently and satisfying expected levels of productivity.

CALVIN:   I think Dana's point is that you're referring to the immediate, tangible stuff we can easily measure. Here's another question for you. How you would define value?

NANCY:   I would define value as positive return.

CALVIN:   Makes sense. And what do you mean when you say positive return?

NANCY: That depends. There is quantitative value, which is I put in a dollar, and I get two back. And there is qualitative value, which is something like I put in a dollar, I win a customer who will spend more than a dollar.

CALVIN: If we put in a million dollars today and receive an additional one percent of market share tomorrow, and that was our target, would you consider that a valuable investment?

NANCY: If we hit the target, one would have to say yes.

CALVIN: What if the one percent of market share only provided us an additional half-million dollars, and we spent a million to achieve it? If we were to do that repeatedly over time, would it lead to long-term health for the company?

NANCY: I suppose not.

CALVIN: I think you'd have to say it wouldn't.

NANCY: I guess that's right.

CALVIN: I always find it interesting to talk about value with other finance people, because we like cold, hard data, stuff we can put into formulas and equations. But here's another scenario. Let's say we make back those two dollars from the one, but we missed a different opportunity that could have earned us three dollars instead of two for the one invested.

NANCY: I'm not sure I understand.

CALVIN: I'll put it a different way. Let's say we can invest the dollar today, and from it we can get two dollars tomorrow or a new customer next week. How would you decide which one to pursue?

NANCY: I would ask how much that new customer is likely to spend.

CALVIN: Great question. Would you ask anything else?

NANCY: Well, I'd also ask whether the two dollars tomorrow would turn into the three dollars next week, or whether it might turn into more. Or less.

CALVIN: And those aren't easy things to calculate, but they certainly help paint a more comprehensive picture. I have to get on a call now, but let's make this a continuing dialogue, okay?

NANCY: Yes. Thank you.

## Questions We Asked

1. Have you ever been challenged to define value? What did you say?
2. Have you ever been asked to imagine different scenarios of investment versus return on behalf of the company? What transpired?
3. Have you ever been asked to think beyond your own area of functional expertise? If so, how 'difficult' or 'unpleasant' did you find it to leave your area of expertise? How did you deal with this?

## Comments We Got

Nancy already began to frustrate many of our participants in this, her second conversation with Calvin, because while she appeared to listen to his words and accept the possibility of an ongoing discussion about defining value, people also expressed a collective opinion that someone needs to shake her up and make her realize that she doesn't necessarily know as much as she may believe she does. Much concern was expressed about Nancy's potential ability to stick with the dialogue Calvin is initiating and ultimately benefit from it. Most people wondered whether she will be able to break out of her current mode of thinking and adopt a new perspective.

Here are the five themes that came out of the comments we received, along with a number of illustrative statements.

1. **Value decisions must incorporate multiple perspectives.**

    'Driven by cost-centre thinking, one cannot see beyond his own cost centre.'

2. **Value is forward-looking.**

    'Tangible financial benefits can generally be calculated. Longer-term synergies or intangible benefits are less easy.'

'In my company, value comes in two flavours: value to the patient in treatment terms (I am in pharma) and value to shareholders in profits. But it has always been in terms of paper money, not free cash flows.'

'Our new definition of value is about creating short-term cash as well as long-term sustainable profits. This is easier to grasp and helps our managers present business cases in a much more realistic way as, in the end, they need to understand that value creation is much more than just one number.'

'Our value definition has an element of creation, transfer and sharing, in a sustainable form. We should not create while destroying what we have. We should be able to transfer back some of what we created to the party for whom we started the project. And we should be able to share part of what we created to keep us going.'

## 3. Value decisions need to be articulated and justified.

'The challenge is not in making sure our projections are realistic, but in getting leadership to understand the numbers and their sources. In other words: managing expectations.'

'I've frequently been asked to come up with different scenarios that made no sense or had no material probability of occurring. However, I felt it was a mandatory step to convince stakeholders to proceed with the investment.'

'The most challenging part is the 'what-if' scenarios our shareholders ask to see before committing to an investment. It is hard to build up models on scenarios that operationally make no sense but that you need to build to satisfy the nervousness of an investor.'

## 4. Value is money – but not just immediate money.

'There are both qualitative and quantitative aspects to value. The qualitative one should be captured by the quantitative one.'

'Value for me is more than financial value. It stretches across the organization from customer to colleague.'

'I've interviewed hundreds of fund managers claiming to have a value approach. Almost all of them had a different definition, which is somewhat strange, as any asset only has only one value. It scares me when people start to use adjectives like "qualitative" to describe value. Cash is what a company needs – nothing more, nothing less.'

## 5. Seeing value means letting go of what you know.

'I was initially afraid to exit my comfort zone; then motivated to explore new territory while seeing how I could apply my experience and knowledge to the new situation.'

'I experience a great deal of discomfort when I have to spend time outside the area in which I'm expert. But this results in a positive surge of energy that I use to do the homework I need.'

'While it's outside of the comfort zone, I find it enjoyable to learn other areas while being asked to contribute to the greater good.'

'Outside of my functional area, I often feel my words are surface and high-level, without substance. As a general manager, you have to listen carefully what your staff in the subject area have to say, and ask the right questions.'

'In the beginning, being out of my functional expertise made me insecure, and I became more of a listener than a contributor. I've since learned that what initially made me change behaviour was that I better prepared for these meetings, having spent more time digging into the material.'

'Not difficult to think beyond my area of expertise; difficult to act beyond my area of expertise, or to think in a different way about my own area of expertise. This feels more comfortable for me when I feel I'm allowed to make mistakes, and I am supported by colleagues and management.'

## Our Thoughts

This time, Calvin smartly schedules a discussion with Nancy alone, so that he can talk to her directly without her being potentially put ill at ease by Dana's highly assertive manner. Calvin slowly opens Nancy's eyes to a way of thinking about value that is far less black-and-white than she's used to, and in so doing he makes her start to consider the implications of making decisions based on definitions of value that may be too narrow, too simple or too short-term focused. Calvin chooses a set of examples that he hopes will begin to illustrate to Nancy that value is not something one defines in a KPI. The value of any decision is based not only on the returns generated by that decision, but also by the opportunities foregone by making it. This is a much broader definition of value than Nancy is used to, and she is having great difficulty grasping its implications.

Nancy, it seems, has a hill to climb. She seems polite and accommodating, but perhaps only half-heartedly so. Coming from a role that was mostly non-collaborative and required her to make decisions largely in a vacuum, Nancy appears to find all this talking about value and exploring the deeper meaning of it vaguely unwelcome, as evidenced by her stiff manner and very careful tone. Transitioning to the role of GM requires not just a gradual alteration of thinking, but an immediate gear-shift. The higher you rise in the organization, the bigger the implications for every decision you make, facilitate, oversee or influence. And the leap from functional manager to GM is, in terms of mentality, the biggest one you will make. It seems that Nancy, at least for now, is still partially stuck in her old ways and unwilling to dive in. She has a generous boss, but a smart one. She will have to change to succeed in this role, and that change will need to happen soon.

**Your Thoughts**

# HUGO

## The Scenario

*After his first executive team meeting, Hugo met with Dino, his boss, who recognized Hugo's discomfort after he had offered an opinion in the meeting that seemed not to resonate with any of the others present. Dino talked to Hugo about his need to acquire a broader perspective as part of his transformation into becoming a general manager, which seemed to mystify Hugo somewhat. Dino told Hugo he needed to move on from becoming a functional expert and instead start thinking of himself as a facilitator of value on behalf of the organization. Hugo was willing to listen, but he was also having trouble understanding.*

*Now, Hugo receives a meeting invitation from Dino with the subject line, 'The journey begins!' Here's how their conversation goes:*

DINO:     *(gesturing toward a series of letters written on the whiteboard)*: Do you know what this stands for?

HUGO:    No.

DINO:     Remember I said you should start thinking of yourself as someone who creates value for the company, rather than making decisions from a marketing perspective?

HUGO:    Yes.

DINO:     I want to help give you some concrete tools for doing that. *(Dino points to the whiteboard again)* This stands for Discounted Expected Free Cash Flows.

HUGO:    Discounted Expected ...

DINO:     Discounted Expected Free Cash Flows.

HUGO:    Discounted Expected Free Cash Flows.

DINO:     For us to be sustainable, we have to think big picture and long term. This is a concept that goes beyond the usual variables and forces us to consider others. It boils down to this: when we're considering doing something, is it going to create long-term value or is it not?

HUGO:    That seems like a simple question.

DINO:    I agree. But it's tough to answer, since it requires people to look at all the relevant factors. In general, they don't. Why?

HUGO:    Because they're looking at the business from a narrow perspective.

DINO:    Right. Either a departmental perspective, or a short-term perspective, or whatever. Companies that have success over the long term understand value conceptually, but they also make decisions about it based on an intelligent analysis of real factors – not just the usual, easy-to-observe ones. Understand?

HUGO:    Not really.

DINO:    Let me put it this way. When you were Marketing Manager, did you feel you were privy to the reasons why the company spent money or made certain investments?

HUGO:    No.

DINO:    Well, the good news is, now you're going to be. The bad news is you're going to need to tell me whether you think those reasons are good or bad.

HUGO:    And not just from a marketing perspective.

DINO:    Exactly. I'm never going to tell you what to think, because I want unbiased views. But I do want to give you some tools to help back up the things you're going to tell me. If we're going to try to accurately assess investment decisions, we need proper data, and rigorous analysis of it. In other words, we need to estimate the true expected benefit. That means weighing all the factors, not just the ones we know will make it look good or bad. It needs to be a completely objective exercise. So – feel like you're ready to start talking about the Discounted Expected Free Cash Flows?

HUGO:    No time like the present.

DINO:    The number one rule is what I said about considering all of the factors. What's the main reason people want to make quick decisions?

HUGO:    They want to look like they're taking action?

DINO:    Sure. What's another reason?

HUGO:    They want to realize the benefits quicker.

DINO:     Right. And in that vein, I'd add a third reason. It's easier to look at a convenient measure, like revenue, and use it to justify the decision. 'Hey, guys, this is going to make us ten million over a three-year horizon, so we should do it.' See the problem with that, though?

HUGO:    Well, it doesn't take into account other variables.

DINO:     Such as?

HUGO:    Cost.

DINO:     And?

HUGO:    Time.

DINO:     And?

HUGO:    Other resources.

DINO:     Now we're getting somewhere.

## Questions We Asked

1. In your company, what are the usual factors used to determine investment decisions? Do they usually yield what you would call positive results?
2. How confident do you feel justifying the reasons behind whether to make an investment or not?
3. Have you ever been asked to make a thorough long-term value assessment on a potential investment decision? How challenging did you find it?
4. Have you ever tried to present the case that a new type of analysis needs to be introduced to your company's decision-making process? How did you make the case? Were you successful? What were the key success factors in getting others to support your proposal?

## Comments We Got

The participant community used Dino's discussion with Hugo as a jumping-off point to enthusiastically describe the ways in which value is assessed and used in their organizations. There was fascinating variety in the replies we received, with some people telling us that their companies are on the ball when it comes to defining and using value, and others grudgingly reporting that their organizations wouldn't know value if it slapped them in the face.

Equally interesting were people's stories of how their company culture approaches value and correspondingly promotes or derails it. In some cases, they said that senior management is receptive to properly considered arguments for a given investment; in others, that the arguments are constantly adapted *post hoc* to an investment decision already made (which usually means sent down from upper management). In the end, our participants showed us that there are many different ways to look at value, but they seemed to agree on one thing in general: ignoring it is not an option.

Four distinct themes came out of the overall responses received. Here they are, with representative comments included.

1. **To assess the value impact of a decision, one must incorporate multiple perspectives.**

   'Most of the time, important decisions are complex and unique. It is therefore important to obtain support from multiple stakeholders through underpinning proposals from several relevant perspectives.'

   'Investments are made after consultation with many stakeholders.'

   'I love the process of Q and A and find it essential to get all subjectivity out of a decision.'

2. **Value-based decisions need to be articulated and justified.**

   'You can always come up with the scenario that justifies the investment by changing the assumptions.'

   'We were recently asked to analyse the potential acquisition of a small Chinese service company. The market was underestimated by our German colleagues, as the dynamic of the

Chinese market is still strange to some. In the end, the trust of the CEO in the Asia team and commitment to bring the company forward led to the successful acquisition.'

'It's actually fun if you have a good spreadsheet set up that allows you to compile different cases with different probabilities. The time spent is "raw material" when it comes time to get presentations or other discussions together. It becomes much easier to understand the overall picture when you spend time throwing rocks at the case to ensure it's the best estimate you can make.'

'For small investments, sometimes gut feeling is okay; for bigger investments, justification by data is more comfortable.'

'Gut feeling seems to play a role in smaller investments.'

### 3. Value is difficult to quantify.

'We make investment decisions based on how our investments will contribute to our results, which are sometimes non-financial and instead related to social change.'

'Clearly financial metrics play a vital role. However, our risk appetite is also important – low risk, quick wins. Social and sustainable goals are becoming more important, but there is generally a financial element involved at some stage, even if very long-term.'

### 4. Value is forward-looking.

'I share my assumptions and have a risk-mitigation plan in case specific elements work out differently than planned. It works well as long as you work as a team, with members you can trust – that is, people who aren't chasing short-term objectives.'

'The big challenge is always discussing the short-term impacts of a long-term projected yield. This is where we need to build the argument block by block, ultimately towards a consensus on the projected value generation.'

'I've started to discuss the idea that we need to stop using WACC for the discount factor and instead use OCC. It's a little rocky, given that I'm a chemical engineer telling a finance guy that there's a big difference between OUR cost of capital and THE cost of capital. One letter I've taken to showing to many people in our office is Warren Buffett's 2013 letter to Berkshire Hathaway's shareholders. There's a quote I love, "If you are a CEO who has some large, profitable project you are shelving because of short-term worries, call Berkshire. Let us unburden you." The idea is that we aren't capital-constrained, we're idea-constrained. I would say that if you invest capital and it doesn't return, it's not the discount's fault, it was probably a bad idea to begin with, and the case was likely full of bad assumptions. I'm still working on this...'

## Our Thoughts

Recognizing that Hugo is receptive to learning, Dino now tries to introduce to Hugo the concrete tools he will need in order to assess and deliver value to the organization. Dino is conscious not to throw Hugo fully into the pressure-cooker of finance at this point. He starts instead by having a general conversation with Hugo about the idea of the Discounted Expected Free Cash Flows, and asks him to consider the various factors that go into estimating it as closely as possible. As before, Hugo isn't exactly brimming with confidence in his ability to absorb and execute the lesson. But, as before, he is a willing student, which at this point is more important.

Dino's explanation of value begins where Calvin's story to Nancy left off. Value is not something we have the luxury of defining ourselves, nor is it a vague notion of qualitative or strategic outcomes. In fact, value is something that can be defined quite concretely, and is entirely consistent with the long-term health of the company: the Discounted Expected Free Cash Flows generated by a decision. It is important to note that, while value is not difficult to define, it is exceedingly difficult to measure. This has significant implications for the general manager and is central to the debate over KPIs. We will speak more about it later.

To fully understand this definition, let's start with the Free Cash Flows. Value is defined in terms of future free cash flows generated by the decision. How far into the future? Indefinitely. This is the long-term perspective of which we speak, and it takes into account, as a definition at least, all of the strategic and long-term societal implications of the decision, as reflected in the company's customers' continued willingness to pay for the goods or services they provide, the regulator's willingness to continue to allow the company to conduct business and any effects of overall societal pressures on how the company will conduct its business. Thus the concept of long-term sustainability is built into the definition of value.

The second term that needs to be clarified is 'expectation'. Expectation refers to the fact that, of course, any future free cash flows are going to be uncertain, hence, at best, we can only talk about Expected Free Cash Flows. Here it is critical to understand the difference between expectation and prediction. This difference is easily illustrated with an example of a coin toss. If I toss heads, the decision will result in a free cash flow of an instantaneous one-time payment of $150, but if I toss tails, the decision will result in an instantaneous one-time payment of $50. (We can ignore the concept of discounting future free cash flows for the moment.) Assuming a fair coin, the expected free cash flow is $100. Note that this is a mathematical concept, as in no instance would the actual free cash flow be $100.

Thus, expectation is not the predicted outcome, but simply a representation of the various possible outcomes ($150, $50) multiplied by their probabilities of occurring (0.5, 0.5). The reason this is a useful representation is that, over a large number of coin tosses, the average should be very close to the expectation. In a corporate setting where many value decisions are made every day, the average of the outcomes over time would be well represented by their expectations.

This concept, possibly even more than discounting, has profound implications for general managers and their approach to managing for value. Expectation is not prediction. This should be written down on a piece of paper and placed on the wall of every GM's office (or better yet, make it your screen saver). To illustrate this concept further, consider that the same coin flip required an investment in order to receive the uncertain free cash flow. If the decision required an investment of $110 and the outcome happened to be heads, did you create value because you received $150? If the decision required an investment of $90 and the outcome happened to be tails, did you destroy value because you received only $50? To answer this question based on value, simply ask yourself, 'Would I make the investment again a thousand more times?' That is, would you agree to run the coin toss one thousand times if you had to pay $110 each time? Would you agree to run the coin toss one thousand times if you had to pay only $90? One creates value only when the expectation of the outcome, appropriately discounted in the case of future free cash flows, is greater than the investment required. General managers who think in these terms create the greatest value in the long run for their companies.

The final concept that needs to be defined is discounting, and this refers back to the idea Calvin was trying to introduce to Nancy earlier. Discounting expected future free cash flows simply reflects the fact that value will always be defined relative to the opportunity costs of a decision. If I take this course of action, make this decision, invest this money, what courses of action have I given up? We can illustrate this with a slight modification to the coin flip example. Instead of the pay-off being instantaneous, let us assume that the pay-off occurs in a year's time. I pay $90 now, toss a coin, and then receive $150 a year from now if it lands heads and $50 if it lands tails. We know now that the expected free cash flow is $100, but we now must wait a year to collect. In defining value, we must account for the fact that the $90 could have been put toward some other opportunity, and that by investing in this particular coin toss we are not investing that same $90 in the other opportunity.

With well-functioning capital markets, there are a tremendous number of alternative investments for the $90, and thus the opportunity cost does not depend on only our opportunities – that is, the opportunities we can create within our company – but the opportunities that exist across all companies and across all markets. This is referred to as the opportunity cost of capital (OCC), and it reflects the expected percentage returns from an investment of similar market risk. The risk does not depend on our own unique risk tolerance, or on any unique, diversifiable risk of the investment, but to the overall risk tolerance of the capital market and the non-diversifiable risk of the investment.

Instead of comparing the $90 investment today to $100 next year, then, we must first discount the $100 by the OCC to arrive at what is called its present value. This is where the term Net Present Value (NPV) comes from: it refers to the present value of the expected free cash flow net of the investment. If the OCC were 12%, then the discounted expected free cash flow would be $100/1.12 = $89.29. Since NPV in this case is less than the $90 investment, it would thus be a value-destroying decision – you paid more for the investment than it was worth. Companies do this all the time in buying up other companies, claiming that the investment has strategic value. But strategy only has value to the extent that it impacts expected future free cash flows.

The good news, Dino tells Hugo, is that he is now going to find himself in the know – no longer a passive recipient of big decisions but part of the inner sanctum, someone privy not only to the decisions themselves but also to the reasons they are being made. However, along with this enjoyable step, says Dino, comes a new responsibility for Hugo: needing to explain, thoroughly and persuasively, why he agrees or disagrees with those decisions. Hugo, to his credit, has listened to everything Dino has said thus far, as evidenced by his immediate response: 'And not just from a marketing perspective.' He hears what Dino is telling him and has expressed an understanding that it is essential for him to leave behind everything that, ironically, has allowed him to ascend to this level of the organization. This version of Hugo, he is quickly learning, has virtually nothing to do with the previous one.

**Your Thoughts**

\* \* \*

## Overall Discussion

Consistently profitable businesses do two things: they understand value conceptually and they apply it with practical rigour. Understanding one's role as a new GM is only half of the initial battle. Understanding first how to define value, and second how to calculate and capture value, is the other half. Myopic businesses make short-sighted or narrow-minded decisions, believing that value is contained only in the tangible, short-term indicators they see in front of them every day. Value-based organizations, on the other hand, look deeper and wider, incorporating all relevant factors – to the extent they are able to form expectations about them – into value assessments. These organizations understand that it is not the final value number on a page or in a spreadsheet that matters, but the process by which they develop those numbers. You can bet they have a good explanation for why they arrive at the investment decisions they do.

In the previous chapter, our GMs realized, in different ways, that they were going to have to change the way they think about themselves and their contribution of value to the organization. In this chapter, they begin to see that discussions about value must be well supported and substantiated, and that no one is going to spoon-feed them the right argument. They are coming face-to-face with the stark reality that translating the idea of sustainable business into long-term, big-picture value is a requirement of every good GM – and that, to succeed in their new roles, they must not only be aware of real value as a concept, but must also be able to bring it to life through tangible data. In learning the importance of capturing value properly, they are also learning the ramifications of not doing so.

In other work, we have carefully explained our own definition of value[1], which we summarize briefly now to clarify this discussion for the remainder of this book. We obtained the 'standard' academic definition of value via a form of backward induction by answering the question, 'What does an organization have to accomplish if it is to survive as an independent entity over the very long term, say a century or longer?'

The answer to this question avoids the common differences of opinion and varied subjective assessment of what value *should* or *should*

---

[1]See, for example, *The Blue Line Imperative: What Managing for Value Really Means* (Jossey Bass, 2013) by Kevin Kaiser and S. David Young.

*not* refer to and focuses instead on an objective understanding of what managing for long-term health really means for a given organization. The answer to this question was eventually determined to be entirely driven by expected cash generation into the future. The important insight is that the survival of the organization doesn't depend upon the decision-maker's own expectations for these future cash flows, but rather on the actual expected (objective) cash flows. This removes the relevance of the subjective assessment of the decision-maker and emphasizes the critical importance of the GM being data-driven and objective in his or her assessment of the future (short-term and long-term) expected cash flow impact of any decision.

However, as any benefit, financial or otherwise, to be received in the future is less valuable than the identical benefit to be received sooner due to the risk of death before delivery of the benefit, as well as due to the risk that the future benefit never materializes as expected, these expected future cash flows need to be discounted to reflect these two facts. Again, in an effort to address the subjectivity of different perspectives on the relative value of future versus present realization of benefit, the field of finance has developed a discount rate concept, referred to previously as the opportunity cost of capital (OCC), which carefully incorporates the risk of death, captured as the *risk-free rate*, and the risk of not realizing the benefit, captured as the *risk premium*.

The combination of these two components of the discount rate equates to our estimate for the OCC. This concept reflects the simple reality that any resources (the 'capital') used in any given pursuit could alternatively have been devoted to another pursuit, thus the opportunity which was passed up determines the 'cost' of the capital engaged for the project. As this idea is independent of the subjectivity of the decision-maker, like the concept of the expected future free cash flows, it simultaneously emphasizes the importance of the GM being sufficiently comfortable with the principles of finance to ensure that decision-making remains oriented around long-term survival (what we refer to as value-based management) rather than short-term targets.

In the Introduction, we asserted that one of the key themes of the journey toward general management involves expanding one's scope in two ways: first, from a short-term to a long-term perspective, and second, from thinking about the implications of your decisions not on your previous individual area of responsibility but with respect to the broader impact on the entire organization. Successful general managers go beyond narrow or short-term indicators, since they do not capture the impact on the entire organization or the impact on its long-term health. They maintain an orientation on organizational value. This means a few things. First, it means they define value properly, as the present value of the expected future free cash flows discounted at the opportunity cost of capital. Second, it means they understand that the expected future cash flows are more than just management's estimations – unseen effects in other areas of the business, and in the future, also play a part – hence they promote continuous learning to achieve better and better estimates over time. Finally, it means they resist the enticement to make things 'easier' by defining success according to narrow, short-term indicators.

## Key Questions to Ask Yourself

1. Are you comfortable with the definition of value as 'the concept which, when maximized, ensures the long-term survival of the organization'? Are you aware that this then equates to the more rigourous definition of value for the business as 'the expected future free cash flows discounted at the opportunity cost of capital?'
2. Are you able to continuously, and consciously, remind yourself of the distinction between the indicators used to measure

period-by-period business performance and the value of the organization?

3. Do you seek to drive decision-making around the value impact on the organization, taking into account the many different angles from which any given decision can ultimately impact value?

4. Are you able to communicate the rationale for value-based decision-making to those around (above, below, alongside) you in your organization?

# Chapter 3

## Befriending the Numbers

### Freddy

#### The Scenario

*In his previous discussion with Trish about the potential Midwest acquisition being tabled by the company, Freddy encouraged a closer look at the numbers surrounding the decision to ensure that it was one that would truly create long-term value for Prism. Trish told Freddy that she recognized he was getting at something, but he needed to try to articulate his argument better to really be heard. She asked him to take some time to look into the details and come back to her with a more fleshed-out view.*

*Freddy knocks on Trish's door. She tells him to come in. Here's what happens:*

TRISH:    I've been thinking more about our discussion regarding the company strategy. I don't want to dismiss your argument, but I'll be honest, Freddy, I don't really know what your argument is. When I say we need to steady the ship, you ask vague questions about long-term value, but I'm not sure what it is you're saying. I'm challenging you to make it clearer.

FREDDY:  Trish, I think this company has done a lot of things over the past decade because people at the top are short-term focused. And now we're fighting for our lives. Truth is, I have a family to support and I don't want to be out of a job in a year because we're going to keep making decisions the same old way.

TRISH:     What's the same old way?

FREDDY:  Through specific, narrow lenses. We can talk tech, we can talk ops, but numbers can tell a story, and my sense is that we don't dig deep enough into those numbers. You said we need to make good arguments for what we recommend. I don't think we can do that by talking about things in a short-term context. If we survive for a year, what's the difference in the end?

TRISH:     But if we don't survive the short term, there is no long term to discuss.

FREDDY:  I'm just saying short-term fixes are useless if they don't contribute to long-term health. If you're riding a bike and the chain falls off because it's faulty, you can put it back on and it might let you ride another block, but it's going to keep falling off.

TRISH:     What solution are you proposing?

FREDDY:  I'm not proposing a solution. I'm proposing a different way of looking at decisions.

TRISH:     A different way?

FREDDY:  A more sophisticated way.

TRISH:     You have a more sophisticated way?

FREDDY:  Not one I can articulate. IT has always come naturally to me, and I'm sure Ops has always come easy to you, but neither one of those tells the whole story when it comes to a given decision. Finance can help us make better decisions. If we're really serious about promoting long-term value for the company, we need to embrace the numbers behind the numbers.

TRISH:     How do you suggest we do that?

FREDDY:  By learning from those who know. What if we were to go on a departmental retreat or something, focused on finance? Bring in a couple of the senior people from Finance and ask them to give us a two- or three-day tutorial.

TRISH:     What for?

FREDDY:  So that everyone can get more comfortable with data. So we can explain the reasons behind what we suggest, and not shut down when others explain their reasons if those reasons are finance-based. If we can't speak that language, the dialogue is over before it starts.

TRISH:      That sounds like a lot of time and resources.

FREDDY:  It is. It's an investment for the future.

TRISH:      How do you think our Ops and IT colleagues would feel about going to math camp?

FREDDY:  I think they'd hate it. You can tell them it was my idea.

TRISH:      You can count on it.


## Questions We Asked

1. In your current role, how often do you need to discuss finance-type analyses to justify decisions? How comfortable or uncomfortable are you with it?
2. Have you ever been in a situation where you 'lost' a discussion because someone else in the room was better able to speak to the data? How did you respond or adjust?
3. Have you seen, or do you often see, decisions being made with a short-term view, to the potential long-term detriment of the company's value?


## Comments We Got

Not surprisingly, Freddy's suggestion to Trish to run a mini finance camp for the department elicited numerous impassioned opinions from our participants. For the most part, people admired Freddy's coming clean with Trish that he himself doesn't have the goods to know enough finance himself, or to teach it to others, in order to make the right argument to upper management, but that he wanted to acquire a minimum amount of proficiency with the numbers to do so. Many of our participants admitted to moments when they felt lost, confused or edged out of an important discussion because they didn't have the right financial knowledge, or even the right lexicon, to be able to participate effectively.

In the same vein, a number of people spoke of having forced themselves to get cozy with finance, even if it wasn't an easy or comfortable thing to do. Some accomplished this by educating themselves privately; others, by initiating training programmes within their companies or departments; and others still, by seeking individual mentors. As a group, our participants agreed almost unanimously that, to succeed at the GM level, if you can't make nice with the numbers, you are ultimately going to find yourself on the outside looking in.

The remarks we received in response to Freddy's scenario converged around six separate themes. Here they are, including some representative comments.

**1. Being a manager sometimes means asking for financial help …**

'While I might get lost on occasion, I will also seek clarity at a later stage so I am clear on the issue, especially if I am in a position of leadership.'

'Several times, I have felt uncomfortable and lost during financial discussions. I learned that I needed to spend more time analysing data and getting a deeper knowledge in finance. Others are in the same boat. We are now offering training in finance for all new managers and anyone with a P&L responsibility, so that everyone can speak the same language.'

**2. … until you can get comfortable with the numbers.**

'I have learned to get comfortable with it and actually impose it as essential part of any decision-making.'

'Time and homework make new things more comfortable.'

'I cannot insist enough on the necessity to debate both the short-term impact and the long-term benefits of a strategy and give both the same attention. Overlooking one over the other will result in deteriorating support from team members during the life of a project if they do not buy into the short-term impact and accept it for the long-term benefit.'

'When I've lost numbers debates, it was usually due to a lack of preparing – looking at the data and then asking questions about it. What assumptions are built in? What if growth doesn't materialize? Why is that number there?'

## 3. Long-term value isn't always easy to explain – which is why you have to be able to explain it really, really well.

'It's important to show how long-term value creation usually provides better return on the invested capital. You cannot simply talk to the void and expect people to believe you.'

'I find short-term impacts quite easy to explain. Longer-term impacts, which are often more intangible, I find less easy to explain, and therefore less easy to push.'

'In my monthly meetings, I have introduced a financial training session called "Financial Freshener" to bring everybody to a sufficient level of financial literacy.'

'When you don't know your data, you feel pressured, and you can just shut right down.'

'When the private equity team did their due diligence on our company, there was a heated debate and I fell short due to a deficient financial vocabulary. I realized the importance of being able to interpret the numbers behind the numbers, as Freddy said it, and then to articulate that interpretation effectively.'

## 4. Even when you're good at explaining the numbers, you have to make sure they're the right ones.

'Some people can do magic with data. If they are the right or wrong data is another discussion.'

'We used to utilize a spreadsheet for financial analysis, but now all transactions will be required to be analysed by the large and complex financial model.'

## 5. Numbers don't always tell the whole story.

'We often discuss the finances of initiatives, but we are more and more moving away from talking about numbers and more toward the logical steps and strategies behind them. The

problem I have seen with numbers, particularly NPV calculations, is that they rely heavily on assumptions that can be
manipulated. It's hard to compare NPVs when you don't know
which of them are realistic.'

'Logic still wins in the end.'

## 6. Be wary when the data is used to sell short-term wins.

'Though I see it less than I have in the past, there is still the
"We need to hit the numbers this quarter" mentality. In some
respects, it does make you wonder whether it wouldn't be better to be a privately-run company just so that you could escape
some of the short-term pressure from Wall Street.'

'I've seen focusing on short-term wins at long-term costs quite
often, not only with the usual references to stock-markets' or
investors' immediate expectations but more often due to difficulties in coming up with valid long-term models and fact-
based hypothesis which go beyond simple assumptions.'

'Short-term success can make one easily forget the long-term
view.'

'When people are not managed with long-term value, they execute their job on a short-term basis. I observe short-term
behaviour destroying long-term value on a daily basis. Starting with myself.'

'Careful when subjectivity takes over data analysis. That's when
long-term sustainability becomes compromised.'

'Long-term value is not always visible in innovative matters. Who
would have known that we would all be using smartphones
with apps today? The data may have been there showing long-
term value but, for companies like Nokia, the implementation
was wrong.'

'Incentive structures are often poorly constructed, where it is
much easier to measure short-term numbers than long-term
value. And you get what you measure.'

'Decisions sometimes perceived as 'short-term' actually take into
account longer-term views, but for management to ensure

people embrace the idea or the change, they emphasize the short-term part in order to create initial momentum.'

## Our Thoughts

Freddy's conversation with Trish reflects the thoughts of many people in his position, even though not all of them are comfortable admitting to their boss what Freddy is admitting to Trish: that he needs to get better with data in order to help articulate the arguments sitting hazily in his head. With Trish's guidance, Freddy is becoming aware that his instinctive understanding of long-term value needs to be backed up by numbers. He can be certain that any investment decision he might wish to challenge will have numbers backing it up, and he has to be prepared to back up his counter-perspective with numbers showing the implications of this perspective on the long-term health of the company.

GMs must indeed do more than offer persuasive words or compelling ideas; they must, to every extent possible, support those ideas with facts and data. Freddy, to his credit, understands this, and also recognizes his own strengths and shortcomings. This combination of self-awareness and willingness to admit where he needs to boost his skills puts him in a good position to help not just himself, and not just his boss, but the organization at large.

It is a benefit to Freddy that Trish seems open to at least this level of dialogue around the issue. Though in previous meetings she has given the distinct impression that her focus is on short-term wins or immediate fixes, it appears she is willing to listen to Freddy's suggestion that the entire department would benefit from cozying up to the numbers. She pushes back a little in response to Freddy's idea that a few individuals from Finance run them through a mini Finance boot camp, but she doesn't reject it. In fact, she seems to tentatively accept the idea – even though she does carefully insert a joke at the end of their chat indicating that it will be made clear to others that it was Freddy's idea. This may simply be Trish's way of covering herself in advance, or it may be her subtly communicating to Freddy that he is now going to take on greater responsibility and visibility for his decisions. The two intentions may be intertwined.

Freddy thus faces a dual challenge: building his finance skills, and continuing to draw Trish over to his side of the fence, where a focus on future vision and the company's long-term health are paramount. Trish seems to be of mixed motivations. Privately she may be hoping to ride out Prism's short-term storm in order to satisfy some unspoken personal agenda – getting to retirement, perhaps, or hoping to be poached by a competitor. But she also clearly allows Freddy regular openings to assert his point of view that the company can only thrive if it creates sustainable value. She may be experiencing an internal battle between her own individual desires and a more altruistic investment in Prism's long-term success. Freddy isn't likely to discover her personal inclinations, at least not in full, so his best approach is to continue to do what he is doing: argue firmly for the importance of value, but tighten his argument and focus it as much as he can around data and facts, so that it has the best chance to resonate not only with Trish but also any other internal audience she is willing to put him in front of.

**Your Thoughts**

## Nancy

### The Scenario

*Previously, Nancy and Calvin spoke one-on-one about the subject of value and its implications for the health of the company. Calvin gently but firmly tried to get Nancy to see through the lens of her colleague, Dana, at least as a means of taking into account all perspectives and broadening her point of view, whether or not she agreed with Dana's specific ideas. Calvin suggested to Nancy that value is not something a manager defines in a KPI, but is defined more broadly in terms of the range of opportunities outside the manager's narrow view of the world.*

*Nancy receives a meeting invitation from Calvin with the subject line, 'Time to play a game'. She arrives at his office. Here's how the conversation goes:*

CALVIN: I wanted to continue our discussion on defining value. I was hoping you wouldn't mind if we did a little numbers exercise together.

NANCY: That sounds fine.

CALVIN: See this coin? Pretend you get $50 if this lands on heads and $150 if it lands tails. I want to know how much you'd pay to play.

NANCY: I'm not sure.

CALVIN: Okay, different question. You don't pay to play. But how much would you expect to win?

NANCY: Well, either $50 or $150, since it's going to result in one outcome or the other.

CALVIN: So, again, how much would you pay to play?

NANCY: I don't know.

CALVIN: What if you get a hundred tosses? Would that change your expectation?

NANCY: I still don't know, because there's no way of predicting the outcome, so there's no way of knowing what I'll get back.

CALVIN: No?

NANCY: I suppose you could take the average …

CALVIN: Which is?

NANCY:    $100.

CALVIN:   If we toss it three times and it comes up heads twice and tails once, what's your average payout?

NANCY:    $50 plus $50 plus $150, divided by three.

CALVIN:   How about if I toss it ten times and seven come up heads? Is the average $100?

NANCY:    No.

CALVIN:   The average isn't $100 unless you've got an even number of tosses and half of them land on each side. Which will virtually never happen in the real world. And, in fact, we don't care what the average is. Know why?

NANCY:    Why?

CALVIN:   Because we want to make decisions based on a best guess of return. Our best guess can't be based on the average, because we can't know it, and even if we did know it for the last hundred tosses, that still doesn't tell us a thing about the next hundred – and it's the future we care about.

NANCY:    How do you predict the future?

CALVIN:   By calculating, as best as we can, what we expect as a return. When you're deciding how much to pay to play this game, sticking to $50 or $150 is most people's instinct, because those seem like the obvious data points. In fact, $100 is what we should expect, and is the number we should base our decisions on. Can I explain why?

NANCY:    Please do.

CALVIN:   Even if the average will hardly ever be $100, if you take the weighted probabilities of all of the potential outcomes, that's exactly what you get. Whether I toss the coin one, ten or a thousand times, the probabilities together yield an expected result of $100. So that's what you expect to get out of this game. Let me ask you again. How much are you willing to pay to play?

NANCY:    Anything less than $100.

CALVIN:   Right. It doesn't matter what you predict the outcome will be. It doesn't matter what anyone predicts. Math tells you the expected outcome, and that's what you have to base your decisions on.

You can't see it and you can't touch it, which makes most people squirm, but it enables a decision based on an objective view of expected value, rather than guesswork. How does that sit with you?

NANCY:    I'm interested in learning more games.


## Questions We Asked

1. How much would you have said you would pay to play the coin toss game at first? Why?
2. Even understanding the logic of the coin toss example, does it make you uncomfortable to think about basing decisions on expected value that you can't 'see'?
3. Can you think of any examples in which people around you have made investment decisions based only on what they or others predicted?


## Comments We Got

Our participants thoroughly enjoyed the discussion between Calvin and Nancy, and had enthusiastic, though not always confident, things to say about how to estimate present investment and future return. People seemed to relate to Nancy's mild anxiety when asked by Calvin how much she would pay to play the coin-toss game, or, separately, how much she would expect to win. The difficulty of answering either question is highlighted by the great variety of the responses we received, many insisting they would not pay more than $50 to play the game, others taking safe harbour around the $100 middle-ground, and still others shying away from the game altogether.

Perhaps more interesting than the variety in our participants' answers was the range of explanations within them. Some people spoke about ignoring one's gut and applying strict logic to estimates of expected return. Others pointed to the importance of weighing averages and calculating probabilities. The extremely honest among our participants chose an answer but admitted they couldn't really explain the rationale behind it. There was one overarching message people seemed to agree on: it can be very difficult to understand the numbers properly, but the more one can do so, the simpler decisions can become – or at least the more confident one can be in making them.

Three particular themes emerged from our participants' reactions to the conversation between Calvin and Nancy. Here they are, along with illustrative comments.

## 1. Predicting outcomes isn't easy.

'I would pay $50 to play the coin toss game. It is not the best expected value, but not the worst either.'

'I would pay up to $100 to play the coin toss game, because that is how much one can win on average.'

'I would pay $100 to play the coin game, since it is the average of the high and low of the two outcomes.'

'I would not pay a dollar more than $50 to play the coin toss game, even though that is surely not enough to participate in the game.'

'I would pay $50 to play the coin toss game. You always get your investment back and have the upside of more.'

'From a gut feeling, I would have opted for less than $50 to play the coin toss game, because then I would always win.'

'You need to pay less than $100 to play the coin toss game. If you pay $100, the NPV is zero.'

'I would pay $50 to play the coin toss game because I would not lose under any scenario.'

'I would pay somewhere between $50 and $65 to play the coin toss, because I would lose little and still have a probability of winning if the $150 materializes.'

2. **Making good financial decisions means first seeing the numbers clearly.**

'Apply logic. Check with others. Create a comfort zone in which to act. When in doubt, get more data or information. Never hesitate to share your doubt.'

'The level of comfort depends on the amount and quality of data available to analyse (or to better "see"), prior to making a decision.'

'The challenge is to leave gut feelings behind and in a purely logical way consider potential outcomes with their probabilities and likelihoods. Then it's just a simple math exercise.'

'The more we support our decisions with facts and data, the clearer we can see the expected result.'

'For a new product launch, we "expected" a certain product to see widespread adoption. We threw a ton of money at it based only on projections – and saw poor results.'

'When you buy an asset with a five-year fixed cash flow, you need to forecast the market level five years later. When the current market is high, people tend to accept the high assumption.'

'This is more about making sure you're making the right decisions. You need to expect that you will get lucky sometimes (and get $150) and be unlucky sometimes (and get $50), but the key is not paying any more than $100.'

3. **Making good financial decisions means relying on both conscious and subconscious assessment.**

'Statistical calculations do not feel "logical" most of the time. Making decisions is done mostly based on expected value that you can't see.'

'I relate this to a lot about how I've spent my own career. I've passed up promotions which would have resulted in more money sooner but more than likely a career flameout when my gut was telling me I wasn't ready or mature enough at that point. I also think of times when I've gone to the mat defending decisions or ideas that were hard to quantify but which I felt would yield a positive return from an expected value perspective.'

'My company did a buyout just before the financial crisis, which turned sour. Signs of a market downturn were there since summer 2007, but everyone was willfully blind.'

## Our Thoughts

Calvin invites Nancy into his office and plays the same game we used to help explain Discounted Expected Free Cash Flows as the definition of value described by Dino to Hugo in the previous chapter. Calvin presents to Nancy what seems to be a simple game involving a coin toss, but which turns out to be a frustratingly difficult exercise in understanding the concept of *expectation* central to the definition of value. If the coin lands heads, Nancy makes $50; if it lands tails, $150. Calvin asks her how much she would pay to play the game, and her reflexive answer is similar to that of most people asked the same question: $50 or $150.

But then Calvin asks Nancy to consider something critical: that this answer reflects our natural human desire to make decisions based on concrete, 'visible' outcomes. The coin-toss question causes difficulty for virtually everyone who is asked it because human nature guides us to play out the story of the coin in our mind. Probabilistic concepts are difficult for us, so we predict the outcome by playing the coin toss in our mind, and in almost every case, we see only $50 and $150. Calvin is trying to get Nancy to acquire a new perspective, one that is often very difficult for people to wrap their heads around: thinking about *expected* rather than *predicted* results.

In the previous chapter, we described how to calculate the expected value of the coin toss using the values of the possible outcomes ($50, $150) and their respective probabilities of occurring (0.5, 0.5), and we discussed why this is a useful definition of value as it relates to the long-term health of the company. When all the probabilities of all possible coin tosses are taken together, $100 is *the* expected return. While any individual can choose to expect whatever they wish, this does not mean that what they expect is actually *the* expected outcome. In the definition of value, the most relevant word is 'the' – as in, **the** expected future free cash flows.

What Calvin is attempting to demonstrate to Nancy with this game is that being a general manager is not simply about having expectations; it is about understanding the business well enough to know what is expected. In the coin toss, any given individual can choose to expect either $50 or $150, but this individual expectation has no impact on the mathematical fact that $100 is the expected outcome.

It is this principle that lies at the heart of managing an organization for long-term health and survival. Calvin is trying to move Nancy away from the relatively comfortable territory of talking about numbers toward the much more anxiety-inducing exercise of using the numbers to make actual assessments about investment and return. The game Calvin asks Nancy to imagine invariably provokes strong commentary on, shall we say, both sides of the coin, because it speaks to an idea that makes many of us uncomfortable: making decisions with uncertain outcomes. The reason the coin-toss game prompts such apprehension is because we can never point to the coin lying on the table after it has been flipped and say we have just earned $100 based on that flip. Each individual instance of playing the game yields a visible outcome of only $50 or $150; it fails to give us a *tangible* argument for basing a decision on an expected return of $100. And because we are more comfortable with things we can touch and explain, like KPIs or short-term targets, we often default to them at the expense of true expected returns.

In moving from the *definition* of value to the *estimation* of value, Nancy must embrace the philosophy that management is not simply about having expectations but about understanding her business well enough to know what is expected. She must be prepared to set aside her opinions and assumptions and focus instead on the objective use of data.

Nancy seems to be coming around to Calvin's point of view. She expresses interest in learning more. As an initial step, this is exactly the attitude she needs to adopt, since, in her new role at The Tipton Group, it will be crucial for her to be able to discuss, and defend, decisions based on expected value. In fact, for Nancy, focusing on a value orientation will be worth a great deal, so that she doesn't allow herself to get distracted by political games or pressure from the likes of Dana. There will be countless moments in which Nancy is faced with an important potential investment decision and asked to determine whether it represents positive or negative value. The sooner she understands what value really means, why it is essential to future success and how to estimate it, the better she will become at making such decisions and being able to justify it as a tool to drive particular actions.

With continued experience, ongoing practice and Calvin's continuing guidance, Nancy will no doubt get better and better at distinguishing decisions that are expected to create value versus those expected to destroy it. If she cannot learn the difference, she will ultimately falter in her new role. But if she can begin to understand where negative value ends and positive value begins, she has taken a vital step toward contributing to the long-term health and success of the business.

**Your Thoughts**

# Hugo

## The Scenario

*In Hugo's previous dialogue with his boss, Dino, they discussed the importance of using data to arrive at sound, justifiable decisions. Dino introduced Hugo to the idea of Discounted Expected Free Cash Flows as a window into a different way of thinking about value – a more complete mentality that goes beyond the usual metrics like revenue or market share. Intrigued by the discussion, Hugo has expressed a desire to learn more. Dino is only too happy to oblige. He sends Hugo a meeting invite with the subject line, 'Careful what you wish for!'*

*Hugo arrives at Dino's office. Their conversation proceeds as follows:*

DINO: So – we talked about DEFCF.

HUGO: Discounted Expected Free Cash Flows.

DINO: How are you feeling about it?

HUGO: It isn't easy.

DINO: Most people think Marketing and Finance are oil and water. Do you agree?

HUGO: I'd say that they're a product of two different instincts.

DINO: And that's why I want to keep pushing you to look at the numbers from a different side. As a marketing expert, you're used to using data as it pertains to customers, market share, and so on. But you're going to need to get comfortable doing things like analysing data from other areas of the business to get the finance perspective – the big picture. Do you know why?

HUGO: Why?

DINO: Because when you're asked to defend certain decisions, you need to be able to explain yourself. I don't need you to become a finance expert, but I do need you to become … unintimidated.

HUGO: I hear what you're saying. We use lots of data in marketing, but finance isn't my strong suit.

DINO: When it comes to value decisions, opinions are worthless. All that matters is trying to figure out what story the data is telling us, and then taking action for the future based on that story.

HUGO:   I have a decent understanding of accounting principles.

DINO:   Be careful. We aren't talking about accounting. Accounting is a record of what's happened in the past. Accounting is, 'We sold 100 units last month at a dollar apiece'. Finance involves making decisions based on an unknown future, and is more complex. Let me ask you this. As a marketing guy, what kind of numbers are you used to looking at?

HUGO:   Sales figures … industry reports …

DINO:   Me, too. We're used to the immediate story – sales by customer segment, by product, by channel. Would you say that's the whole story?

HUGO:   I have a feeling the answer is no.

DINO:   Right. Looking at the bigger picture allows us to make better decisions based on our best read of the data. As an example, I don't ever want you to say: 'We think we should roll out this toy because the focus groups tell us it's a good idea.' It isn't good enough.

HUGO:   But don't you think experience and industry knowledge matter?

DINO:   Only insofar as they enable interpretation of data. If I were CEO, I'd demote anyone who ever said, 'I'm going to go with my gut on this one'. Your gut may know a lot, but it doesn't help others explain why it's a good idea or enable them to challenge you with what their gut says, or the data they might have. A contest between guts has no resolution. But a discussion using actual data and logic does. Knowledge and experience help inform the numbers – and the better informed your data, the better chance you have of seeing the real story.

HUGO:   You talk about it like it's a puzzle to solve.

DINO:   That's exactly how I see it. Imagine every decision as a jigsaw puzzle and the data as the pieces. If you have one piece, it's hard to know what the picture is. If you have half of the pieces, it's easier. If you have almost all of the pieces, you're almost sure to see the whole picture. I never thought of it that way before. Thanks!

HUGO:   My pleasure – I guess.

## Questions We Asked

1. Have you ever been in a position where you had to make a decision on an important investment based on what you felt was limited data? What did you do?
2. Have you ever had to argue against a colleague or superior making what you felt was a misguided 'gut' decision that lacked data to support it? How did you handle the situation?
3. Have you been in a situation where two managers had differing opinions about a particular decision and both were simply insisting on their 'correctness' without providing actual data to support their opposing viewpoints? How was the situation resolved?

## Comments We Got

The conversation between Dino and Hugo elicited an interesting array of responses from our community of participants. A number of people focused on the importance of sticking with the data and ignoring all other factors. Others pointed out that knowledge and experience matter, and can help one determine which numbers are salient in the first place. Most of the views expressed fell somewhere between these two ends of the spectrum. The majority seemed to agree that the ultimate goal is to gather as much relevant data as possible, interpret it impartially, and defend it as best you can. As a collective, our participants also made the frequent qualification that, no matter how well you stack up your argument, sometimes there is no other option than to bow to the influence of those higher up the company ladder.

Three themes took centre stage regarding people's thoughts on Hugo's ongoing situation. Here they are, along with representative comments.

**1. Get as broad a perspective as possible on the numbers to make the best estimate you can.**

  'When there is a decision to be made, I spend a lot of time talking with others, getting a better understanding of the investment and using others' views to support the facts I've been working with.'

'Data is always limited. It is important to make the best decision model and discuss uncertainties and assumptions with the people involved.'

'When not all of the data is available, you have to seek to understand the implications of various decisions and their potential outcomes.'

## 2. Challenging your boss is hard, but sometimes necessary.

'I was asked to support a decision based on my superior's gut feeling, even though the data and facts did not support the decision. To my continuing regret, I gave my support.'

'I gave in to a decision by my supervisor on an acquisition without being convinced, due to lack of analytical data. We have not yet hit the wall on that project, but it is my daily concern.'

'When setting sales objectives, I try to determine realistic and achievable objectives. But the company heads often push unachievable sales objectives. It's very difficult to defend one's POV when the subjective POV is that sales people sandbag, and the only way to get them to do better is to stretch their objectives. Net-net, the bosses win.'

'Recently, my boss made a decision I didn't agree with. My best course of action was to ask him where the numbers came from. When he said, "My gut", I started asking questions. If I didn't know which questions to ask, I would ask people who did know so I could understand the situation better. Maybe his gut is right, but I would want to build the case for myself so I can either talk him out of it or be in a position to better help articulate the case to others.'

'When my superior disagreed with a recommendation of mine, I issued a formal analysis containing a clear list of sources for the data and an endorsement from Finance. It was not a very good way to handle the situation, as I avoided the open conflict, and instead of defending my analysis, merely communicated it.'

'If someone with power has already made a decision for his own reasons, and is just looking for any data or argument to suit or support it, it is almost impossible to reverse.'

'If your superior makes a decision you don't think the data supports, it is important to try to understand why he or she made it. Just throwing more numbers and rational proof onto the table will not lead to a common understanding. It will make you look stubborn, and usually achieve the opposite result.'

'Unfortunately, when the content is unclear, the one who best transfers his confidence level to the audience often wins.'

### 3. You're always guessing to some degree.

'Especially in a true innovation market, data is rarely available at the outset. This is why it is important to work in an agile process, and develop and test fast. But it is still a risky game.'

'The data can't rely on too many unqualified assumptions. I recently tried to challenge the data with Finance and with those who had made similar previous investments. I also tried to build best- and worst-case scenarios, at least to the extent scenarios could be built. We agreed on something in the middle.'

## Our Thoughts

Having given Hugo his insights into the definition of value, Dino now brings the conversation around to estimating value. Dino gives Hugo two specific things to think about in this conversation, both of which will become critical for Hugo to internalize to succeed in his transition from functional expert to general manager (or, as Dino phrased it earlier, 'contributor of value to the organization'). The first of these is the distinction between accounting and finance. Hugo tells Dino that he feels pretty comfortable with accounting principles, but Dino corrects him immediately. Accounting has to do with the past, he says; finance concerns the future. That's why accounting is more tangible. If you sold one thousand units last month, you sold one thousand units, and it is Accounting's responsibility to record that number.

Finance asks you to estimate how many units you expect to sell *next* month, a much more complex task, and one which leads to Dino's second important point, the analogy for which is inadvertently offered by Hugo's casual mention of a jigsaw puzzle. Dino asks Hugo to consider finance decisions in exactly that way – as a jigsaw puzzle which, ironically, is in the end unsolvable, but which it is your task to try to fill in as much as possible before seeing the complete picture.

What you cannot do is snap your fingers and make data available that isn't there. What you *can* do is diligently gather as many pieces of the puzzle as you can, assemble them objectively, invite the unbiased input of others who have done similar puzzles in the past, and then make a decision based on both the limited picture in front of you as well as the pieces you do not have and cannot see. This may sound a little strange, but recall that your approach to problem-solving involves a combination of conscious and subconscious processes. While your conscious processes tend to focus on the visible (in order to be able to explain the outcome of the process and thus be 'aware' of why the decision was taken), your subconscious processes are continuously filling gaps in the data to form a coherent whole, that is, it is taking a more holistic perspective to support decision-making.

The price paid for this subconscious approach is that we are often unable to explain why we consider a decision to be the best, thus others are unable to question our logic. However, the benefit of this holistic perspective is extremely useful in a general management environment, where we are continuously asked to solve the kinds of puzzles to which Dino is referring. Of course, we must also keep in mind that many of the gap-filling efforts of our subconscious process will be accomplished using self-serving biases, of which we must always be aware. We must therefore make conscious efforts to check our assumptions to minimize this downside, while deriving the benefit of the holistic perspective supplied by our subconscious considerations.

This will become especially important for Hugo as he moves from thinking about, and understanding, the numbers himself to discussing and debating them with others. As many of you pointed out, simply being able to speak the language of finance is often a significant part of the battle, regardless of one's talent for interpreting the jigsaw puzzle. In the same fashion, believing that you understand the story the numbers are telling is one thing, but it is only pertinent if you can explain that interpretation to others in a way they can understand. The very effort to explain your perspective to others will help to bring your subconscious process toward the conscious level to help get the benefit of seeing the whole puzzle, while minimizing your individual biases as others challenge your assumptions.

At the moment, Hugo is having comfortable one-on-one talks with Dino in a mostly stress-free atmosphere. Justifying his value-based decisions to others will become a harder task amid the typical pressure-cooker of office politics, corporate bureaucracy and hidden agendas. He will have to learn to take specific analyses, translate them into language others can grasp, and demonstrate to those above, below and lateral the long-term implications for making both kinds of decisions – the ones expected to create value and the ones expected not to.

**Your Thoughts**

*    *    *

## Overall Discussion

As evidenced by the breadth and avidness of the responses we received, finance has a way of getting people wound up. There's a good reason for this. It's hard; and, unlike accounting and its balance sheets, it doesn't give you immediate feedback as to whether you're right or wrong.

Each of our three GMs is starting to tread closer to the numbers – Freddy by suggesting a boot camp hosted by Finance, Nancy by starting to consider the true nature of expected value, Hugo by shifting his thinking about estimates as puzzles to be tackled, even if all the pieces cannot be found at first. All three recognize that they need to build confidence and assurance in their ability to handle data and, moreover, explain their thinking to others. No one likes to be asked to predict the future, which is how many new managers perceive their role. But our new GMs are starting to see, with the help of their bosses and peers, that this is not what general management is asking of them. Rather, successful general management is about seeing the big picture when some of the puzzle pieces are missing, and having a data-driven process for finding as many of those missing pieces as possible. In the end, one must make value-based decisions to support the long-term health of the business, and one must find estimates of expected outcomes to justify those value-based decisions.

It is an essential lesson for our GMs to learn. A proper understanding of value, and sound decisions based on this understanding, can come only from an ability to deal with everyday data. Freddy, Nancy and Hugo come from different backgrounds and bring different competencies to their new positions, but each must develop financial expertise in order to fulfil their managerial roles. To make true value-based assessments and to demand the same of those around them – and thereby to help build sustainable futures for their companies – they cannot shy away from the finance aspect of their jobs. They must come to understand that opinions are dangerous because they are personal, and that what matters is a proper evaluation of the story told by the data, and subsequent actions based on that story.

Freddy, Nancy and Hugo are confronting finance in a way they never had to in their previous roles, except perhaps at a superficial level. To succeed, they must come to understand that finance is intricate, demanding, imprecise, and, while informed by the past, focused on the future. They need to accept that what they see does not necessarily tell the true story of what is expected.

Consider two different golfers. The first makes it his goal to improve his score each round. That is the data point on which he focuses. He pays no attention to the underlying mechanism driving the outcome, his swing. The second golfer ignores his score and instead invests time and energy in refining his swing. The first golfer certainly has an easier argument to make, since he can point to a tangible outcome after every round and easily quantify his progress to others, even if it is the wrong direction. The second golfer has a much harder task in explaining his investment to his golfing buddies, since he believes that the key driver of his score is his swing, which is not measurable. He will not be able to cite an improved score for a while. He may even see his score get worse before it gets better, since anyone who has played golf knows that tinkering with one's swing usually leads to comedy before it leads to success. But the second golfer, if he has identified the underlying drivers of swing success properly, will reap the benefits of his investment for a long time to come. He will have created true value.

## Key Questions to Ask Yourself

1. Are you aware of the difference between what you wish were true and what is actually true?

2. Do you consciously ask yourself which of your assumptions are not actually true?

3. Do you actively seek data and evidence to disprove your most-loved assumptions in order to improve the quality and integrity of your decision-making, or do you selectively focus only on the data which supports your assumptions?

4. Are you comfortable with the difference between predicting future outcomes (which is generally impossible) and forming expectations based on underlying probabilities?

5. Are you comfortable with the difference between having your own expectations for the future of your business and deriving expectations for the business based on what is actually observable?

# Section 2
# Managing Others

# Chapter 4

## Leaving the Nest

### Freddy

### The Scenario

*In his previous conversation with Trish, Freddy continued to argue for long-term value creation and deeper analyses of potential investment decisions, using as a current example the consideration of senior management to acquire the toy company in the Midwest. Trish again told Freddy that she could accept his argument conceptually, but that he needed to make it concrete and specific, supported by data, if he wanted the dialogue to be able to gain any traction – not just with her, but with anyone else.*

*Further to Trish's suggestion to better articulate his position, Freddy prepared an analysis of the numbers surrounding Prism's proposed acquisition of the Midwest toy company. Appreciating the effort he'd made and agreeing with the analysis, Trish allowed Freddy to share it with upper management, with her endorsement. Based on this analysis, Prism has decided to proceed with the acquisition, projecting expected positive return. As a result, Freddy's overall visibility has suddenly increased.*

*Freddy receives a meeting invitation from Trish. It is marked urgent. Their conversation proceeds as follows:*

TRISH:   I wanted to congratulate you on the work you did regarding that acquisition decision. Everyone sees the analysis you did as a major contributing element. It shed light on the numbers in a way people aren't used to.

FREDDY: Thanks. I appreciate your being open to it.

TRISH: That means senior leadership is looking at you in a new way. You're becoming, shall we say, more visible.

FREDDY: What do you mean?

TRISH: Don't worry – it's a good thing. It's good for you and it's good for our department. But I'm wondering how you're handling it with your own team.

FREDDY: Handling what?

TRISH: I guess you haven't heard the comments.

FREDDY: What comments?

TRISH: People on your team are murmuring behind your back. I've heard them.

FREDDY: You have?

TRISH: Oh, sure. In the lunchroom, the bathroom, at their workstations. The funny thing is they're more careful around you than they are around me.

FREDDY: Are they upset?

TRISH: Of course. Upset, jealous, resentful …

FREDDY: Why?

TRISH: Because it's human nature.

FREDDY: What am I supposed to do about it?

TRISH: Nothing.

FREDDY: Nothing?

TRISH: Look, this is going to sound harsh, but you can go up, down or remain stagnant. Which would you prefer?

FREDDY: Obviously up.

TRISH: Well, upward movement carries some stuff with it. Including others sometimes being unhappy. Unfortunately, the only way to avoid company politics is to work for yourself.

FREDDY: That does sound harsh.

TRISH: No one is saying you have to be a different person. Maybe I can help you think about it a different way. You aren't playing games; you're doing valuable work. You aren't being manipulative; you're

trying to improve clarity on important company decisions. Do you
not want to be doing those things?

FREDDY: No. I mean yes. I mean, no.

TRISH: People are going to see it how they see it. Comments are going
to be made. Haven't you ever made comments to your colleagues about me or others above you?

FREDDY: Um …

TRISH: Don't worry, I'm not putting you on the spot! My point is that people are going to make judgements when they see others moving
up. But upward movement is justified if it's a result of hard work
and real contribution of value.

FREDDY: So what are you suggesting?

TRISH: I'm suggesting that you keep doing what you're doing and try to
ignore any noise around you.

FREDDY: What about my peers? What do I tell them?

TRISH: You don't have to tell them anything. Your job is to execute your
role and bring value to the organization. Keep doing that and let
me worry about the rest.

## Questions We Asked

1. What do you think Freddy should do about the comments his
   colleagues are making about his rising profile?
2. Have you ever been in a situation in which your own upward
   advancement was resented by those around you? How did you
   manage it?
3. How can Freddy improve his understanding of how others, especially those on his team, perceive him?

## Comments We Got

As our participants rightly identified as a group, Freddy is now dealing with two issues that invariably go hand in hand: upward mobility within the organization and, as a direct consequence, a changed
perception in the eyes of others. Since Freddy has never occupied

this level before, he is surprised to hear from Trish that this sort of thing is even occurring. His analysis of the investment opportunity has suddenly put him in good stead with senior management, and now he must deal with the unavoidable corollary when it comes to the way people deal with other people, including jealousy, resentment, suspicion and silence.

Many people noted that Freddy has all the opportunity in the world to turn this potential pitfall into a positive. A wide range of suggestions were offered for Freddy to address this sensitive situation head-on. The vast majority felt that he should do so via transparency, honesty, directness and constant communication with, and involvement of, his team. A number of people stressed specifically that Freddy should make a concerted effort to give credit to others whenever possible, in order not to seem as though he is simply trying to satisfy a personal desire to move up. Many felt strongly that he should always strive to involve others on the team so that he doesn't seem like an island to them, and furthermore that he should always be mindful of each individual relationship. Collectively there was strong agreement that, at this juncture in Freddy's trajectory, nothing is more important for him than maintaining the right kind of support from the right people, including those he now manages, his immediate supervisor and the bosses above, who now have him on their radar screen.

Four themes came through strongly in the responses we received. Here they are, with a sampling of individual comments.

**1. Turn attention, and credit, away from yourself ...**
　'If his team helped out on the work he did, he needs to thank them for it and make them visible also. If not, he needs to reassure them that now that he is in a better place to make decisions, he'd like to involve them on projects that are of importance to the company and make them visible for it also.'
　'Freddy should be quick to give credit away – to others, that is.'

'Freddy should help the team members see that the output is a product not just of him but of all of them.'

'He needs to reassure them they are part of the bigger picture and provide ongoing recognition to his team members.'

## 2. ... and maintain the right support.

'He has to be aware of the comments, but should not change his vision/his objectives. Sharing successes, and keeping sponsorship from his boss, are important.'

'The key is to ensure the team have clarity and support you. As you move up, it's vital you continue to have the support of the wider business, including your direct reports.'

'The support I received from my line manager helped me gain confidence in addressing this problem efficiently. I reached out more, I made sure I had my path explained to all those who wanted to listen, and I mentored some who asked for it. Rising upward comes at a price in terms of relationships at work. If those relationships are kept within the work environment and do not extend to the social level, one can manage the negative effects easier. I had made this choice earlier in my career and that made it easier for me to manage resentment on promotion day.'

## 3. Involve and empower those on your team.

'It is important for Freddy not to deviate his focus on his mission, but I do not agree on him going on with it without paying attention to those comments. Each of those making comments have different motives or reasons to follow the trend. I would advise Freddy to engage, communicate and do his best to rally the support of those who are ready to support him. Those are in general the majority who do not have any other specific reason to make those comments other than participating in a discussion. One way to find out is to ask for help from team members, study the response, accept and recognize those who supported him as publicly as possible and share his success with them. Ironically, Freddy's leadership can only weaken if he continues down the same (upward) path without rallying support in his organization.'

'Freddy should do 360° with his team. He should organize one-to-one discussions. He should engage them more in the analysis and decision process. And he should show them the highest possible degree of fairness so that he gains their trust, and they will then in turn engage with him more freely.'

'I am sure Freddy knows his team well enough to approach the one(s) who speaks the most and use them to get conversations started. As time progresses, he can put difficult topics or questions on the table, or even better, encourage others to bring them up. He should have group meetings but also spend time with individuals, asking them to participate in special tasks, etc., so they can feel involved and will get to know him better.'

'Freddy should find ways to involve his staff on new projects, and he should lunch with them one-on-one to hear how they feel and what they expect.'

'There are a lot of behavioural rules Freddy should adopt – being available, giving timely offers of support to those who least expect it, sharing ideas, and asking for opinions in one-to-one situations. All of this will create an environment favourable to detect how others perceive Freddy and how he can better manage the team relationships.'

'Freddy should spend time with the members of his team. One should build good relationships ALL the time, not just when there's something to do. There's a lot of value in talking with coworkers, passing on information, and so forth.'

'I think a big part of why I haven't encountered a lot of resentment when promoted is that I really try to help people by sharing information and knowledge. I really believe that the enemy is other companies, not my co-workers, and so I spend a lot of time communicating, teaching and leveraging things I know to help others. Or people really do resent it and I don't know about it ...'

'Spend time with team members in the office, but outside it as well. It is important to have your team engaged with you.'

'Freddy should indeed thank his team and others who were involved; perhaps there can even be a small celebration. Furthermore, he should continue to keep as many people, including his direct reports and peers, involved in the next steps, explain the overall objectives and continuously check base with all of them if they are all still on the right track. He should make it very clear this is not about him. This acquisition is a company decision for the good of all. Personally, if he's given an opportunity (i.e. one of his co-workers talks to him about it), he should echo some of the same things that Trish told him. That his contributions were just about doing needed work. That he asked questions, and was given an opportunity to try to shed light on those questions.'

## 4. Communicate openly and honestly.

'Nothing he can do about gossip. However, he should remain open to everybody. The higher he climbs, the more he needs help from people around him, so he should be accessible.'

'It's important that Freddy maintains good working relationships through regular communication. A more formal way to do this would be to undertake a 360 degree survey where he will get direct feedback.'

'One important point is to have open and honest communication with your team and ensure that they are part of something. He must lead them, but seeking their opinion/input will also greatly help. Have meetings, yes, but these meeting must be effective and allow open communication. If this does not exist, then you will have difficulties opening up real team spirit. Establishing a speak-up culture is tough, but very valuable.'

'Freddy should and must address openly the comments around him. It is important to have a discussion about the fairness of his promotion and also thank his team. A good manager is only as good as the results delivered by his team.'

'By sharing his thoughts and sincerely asking for those of his colleagues, he can show sincere attention.'

## Our Thoughts

Given his unexpectedly increased profile with upper management, Freddy stands at a sensitive spot. That he is not even aware of it until Trish points it out to him magnifies to an even greater degree how important it is for him to gain an immediate understanding of what he needs to do.

What he needs to do, as Trish astutely makes clear, is invest as much into managing relationships as he invests into doing good work. His analysis of the potential acquisition of the Midwest toy company has alerted others to the fact that he is a valuable asset for the organization. But now he has a separate problem to deal with. The promotion to his current role is already going to have made others consider him in a different way; now that he is getting the attention of upper management, they are going to start treating him even more differently.

Freddy, to his credit, seems to be wholly focused on the work in front of him. As someone with an IT background, it is a good bet that he has not had to spend a lot of time dealing with people issues, office politics or relationship management, at least in his work environment. Trish is telling him something critical. He must continue to do great work, but he also must be an effective leader of people, at a time when they are going to be very careful around him, since he is now the boss. However, he needs to be careful with her final words of advice: 'You don't have to tell them anything. Your job is to execute your role and bring value to the organization.' He needs to have a communication strategy to deal with any rising resentment among his peers, and it is unlikely that the best strategy will be to 'tell them nothing'. Freddy must first accept the fact that he is no longer who he was before. Others will be different around him now because he *is* different. He has both new responsibility and authority, and it is important that he welcomes these and uses them as effectively as possible to be a contributor of value in his management role.

Acting like 'just one of the crowd', though it may be his first instinct, will not prove an effective strategy for Freddy with his former peer group. He is no longer one of the crowd: he is the boss. Consequently, those he manages are going to adopt a completely different attitude toward him, and therefore new behaviours. They are going to be at various times reserved, fearful, skittish or ingratiating.

This is unavoidable, and Freddy must ignore the noise, which can only distract him negatively and, should he engage in it, create a troublesome dynamic between him and those he now must lead. The two most crucial things for him to do are (a) maintain open lines of communication with the members of his team and (b) let them know, through both his words and his behaviours, that he is entirely focused, as they also should be, on making decisions that create value for the company and help contribute to its long-term success.

**Your Thoughts**

## Nancy

### The Scenario

*Two days earlier, Nancy's boss Calvin invited her to his office to play a coin-toss game. He used the game, in which Nancy had to decide both how much to invest and also how much she would expect to win, to impart a basic lesson about expected value – that it is based on the weighted probabilities of all possible outcomes, and should not be confused with anyone's prediction of what will happen. It was Calvin's way of conveying to Nancy that value is not something a manager defines, but it is something that a manager must estimate. Even though one cannot necessarily 'see' expected value, one must spend the time collecting data that allows a fair estimation of it. Nancy understood Calvin's point and expressed enthusiasm in learning more.*

*On the heels of this meeting, Nancy requests a follow-up discussion with Calvin. He is only too happy to oblige. Here's how the conversation goes.*

CALVIN:  Hi, Nancy. You said you wanted to chat about something?

NANCY:  Yes. I wanted to ask your advice.

CALVIN:  Fire away.

NANCY:  I was speaking to my two direct reports earlier. It feels odd, since just a few weeks ago they were my ...

CALVIN:  They were at the same level as you, and now you're above them.

NANCY:  Yes.

CALVIN:  Is that what feels odd?

NANCY:  No, it isn't so much that. It's that, well, we were discussing the company strategy, and when the subject of KPIs and targets came up, something strange happened.

CALVIN:  What's that?

NANCY:  I found myself sounding more like Dana.

CALVIN:  Is that so?

NANCY:  Yes. The more they talked about hitting targets, the more I heard myself talking about creating long-term value.

CALVIN:   Makes sense. You're starting to see through a different lens –
          which is great. But now you have a new situation to deal with.
          The people under you are still worried mostly about getting pro-
          moted. They see the easiest road to promotion as hitting the tar-
          gets that are set for them. That's what they think will get them
          their bonuses and ensure an upward track.

NANCY:    Is it my responsibility to convince them otherwise?

CALVIN:   It isn't entirely your responsibility. Value creation is the responsi-
          bility of everyone in the company, top to bottom. They need two
          things from you. First, they need to know that you don't mea-
          sure their contribution based just on whether they hit targets and
          satisfy KPIs. Second, they need to know that you yourself walk
          the talk.

NANCY:    What do you mean?

CALVIN:   I mean if you tell them it's about more than hitting targets, but your
          own behaviour demonstrates otherwise, there will be a serious
          disconnect in the message you're trying to send.

NANCY:    It sounds like you're telling me to be two different people at the
          same time.

CALVIN:   Not at all.

NANCY:    Or to send two different messages.

CALVIN:   No. I'm saying it's paramount for you to be consistent in the mes-
          sage you communicate now.

NANCY:    Okay. What is that message, and how do I communicate it?

CALVIN:   Well, if you find yourself saying some of the things Dana was
          saying, that must mean you buy into them at some level. Is that
          true?

NANCY:    I believe so.

CALVIN:   If that's the case, then I think the message you're giving yourself
          is one of creating long-term, sustainable value for the company.
          And if you're telling yourself that message, it's the same message
          you should be transmitting to everyone else, in both your words
          and your actions, whether they're above or below you.

NANCY:    What about targets? What about KPIs? What do I say to my
          directs?

CALVIN:   You don't have to explode their ideas overnight. I think what's important is just to get them starting to think about targets and KPIs as part of a bigger picture of value.

NANCY:   As opposed to goals in and of themselves.

CALVIN:   Right. Ideally the targets and indicators we use should reflect our value orientation.

NANCY:   But they shouldn't define it.

CALVIN:   Yes. Now you have to get them to hear those words. And understand what you mean. It won't be easy.

## Questions We Asked

1. What advice would you give Nancy for managing her interaction with the former peers who are now her direct reports?
2. How would you demonstrate a commitment to value in words and deeds if meeting KPIs has been the traditional definition of a positive outcome within the organization?
3. Have you ever had a boss who seemed to change his or her outlook on what it meant for you to contribute in a valuable way? How did you manage this?
4. Have you ever had to change your message to people reporting to you in order to reflect a different value orientation or definition? What were some of the challenges involved?

## Comments We Got

Recognizing the new spot that Nancy now finds herself in, our participants encouraged her to take the bull by the horns by establishing clear messages and behaviours with those who are now her direct reports. People were unanimous in the view that Nancy must transmit very clearly her long-term vision and, even more important, her alignment with the company strategy. We observed strong insistence in the collective belief that Nancy's actions must reinforce this statement to those around her. It was clear in everyone's eyes what Nancy needs to do at this moment in her professional arc: embrace her new role, use it to lead effectively, be clear in her purpose and her vision, and demonstrate exactly the kind of value-creating behaviours that she wants others to emulate.

Participants' responses to Nancy's conversation with Calvin centred around four distinct themes. Here they are.

## 1. Be clear and consistent about your role and your purpose.

'As you take a new position, you need to express your long-term vision and your goals for yourself and the team, defining expectations that align with those of the organization.'

'She needs to make them see that creating long-term value implies not only being ambitious on your own behalf but also on behalf of the company.'

'She needs to make the message clear for herself first. What does she want to stand for, and how does she want to be seen?'

'Calvin has mentioned two key words to Nancy: consistency and behaviour. Nancy, too, was following the KPI route without much attention to long-term value creation. Shifting from one position to the other overnight at the outset of a promotion will definitely not give her any credibility with her new team. She needs to manage her transition by rallying support through communication and sharing on issues such as KPI impact on the company's overall vision and targets, and the rationale behind certain KPI implementation, and she needs to be able to translate to her team part of what she is being exposed to with her new role as a senior manager, and formulate in a clear way how the team efforts in meeting their KPIs can serve the overall purpose of value creation and individual aspirations for career development.'

'It is hard to demonstrate value creation with no data to back it up. KPIs are meant to be that – data – and the action plans used to achieve the targets are equally important.'

'We use KPIs, but we are also strongly driven by value creation, so we treat the KPIs as secondary. Never lose focus on the ultimate goal, and make sure the team does not either.'

'I would start by outlining my expectations, and then try to address any concerns. When I got promoted, I heard from employees that their two biggest concerns were (a) leaders who didn't care about the business and (b) how long I was going to be in the role, since previous leaders had spent an average maximum of just eight months in this job. I addressed (a) by talking to everyone I possibly could associated with the business. My boss addressed (b) by telling people publically that I would be in the role for at least three years.'

## 2. Keep an open flow of communication.

'Express your values. Be open about them. Try to get people on the same page via discussion, though it may take some time.'

'For any changes, however, I always explain to my team the reason and the logic behind. If there is something I do not like but have to accept, I still share it and explain the rationale. It may not be always convincing to my staff, but without it, I cannot run the team.'

'It is the manager's role to communicate quickly with the team. It is also his responsibility to discuss with his superior and share his view, as he needs to be on board with the direction and be convinced that it is the right one.'

'Have a group meeting and discuss the idea that KPIs, while they may have been used as a stick in the past, are now going to be used to help drive business understanding for the primary goal of value creation. You can also drive a bit of ownership and ask whether or not these are the right metrics to be tracking. If they aren't, challenge the group to propose new ones.'

'Comply or explain: if you are doing something different from the defined KPIs/targets, make this clear, explain it well, and make sure that your explanation is related to the long-term objectives of the organization.'

'It's helpful to set up one-to-ones with all direct reports, take people's pulses, and find out what they care about. Having these discussions also communicates their importance to you, as well as giving them a chance to ask you questions.'

'Be honest and open about what you are trying to achieve, and solicit feedback. That's a very powerful tool.'

### 3. Accept that you're someone different; don't shy away from it.

'Keep an open dialogue, but be clear about the changed relationship.'

'It is important for Nancy to realize she is now a manager and she needs to change her behaviour. She needs to define her own message and story instead of relying on someone else's message. The key is also to be consistent in the new behaviour. Also, there is no harm in addressing openly the fact that she was a colleague, but now she is a manager, and ask the feeling of the team as well as remind the team to respect the decisions she will take.'

### 4. Lead by example.

'Nancy needs to walk the talk, showing those around her that she balances long-term value creation with short-term focus.'

'Nancy can build her legitimacy, and thus her authority, by demonstrating actions that help the team and the organization.'

## Our Thoughts

Nancy finds, despite her seeming lack of compatibility with Dana, that she is starting to get more comfortable with the perspective Dana was advocating: that short-term targets and KPIs are useful as tools to reflect the company's orientation toward value, as opposed to self-contained goals in and of themselves. That Nancy is open-minded enough to experience this shift is positive evidence that she has the potential to perform her new role effectively.

But now she has a new problem to face. Those in her charge still think of KPIs and targets as the ways to get promoted and earn year-end bonuses. It is Nancy's responsibility to show them that she is not measuring their contribution based merely on whether they hit targets and satisfy KPIs. Not unlike the circumstances facing Freddy, her challenge now is to demonstrate, in words and deeds, a commitment to acting in the interests of long-term value creation, even though, traditionally, hitting targets and satisfying KPIs have been seen – not just by others but by Nancy herself – as the definition of a positive outcome. Nancy is coming to understand that the ultimate objective for The Tipton Group must be long-term sustainable value creation, which also must be upheld as the ultimate objective for her and her team.

Changing an entrenched perspective is not a quick task, nor is it an easy one. Nancy will do herself and the organization a major disservice by looking at this as an overnight change. She needs to start communicating openly, consistently and frequently with her team to get them on board, and to ensure that they understand and buy into the message of value creation that she herself has absorbed.

**Your Thoughts**

# Hugo

## The Scenario

*In their previous conversation, Hugo and Dino talked further about value. Dino encouraged Hugo to strive to understand the story the data is trying to tell, and he emphasized the difference between accounting – recording what happened yesterday – and finance – using data to make good decisions about what is going to happen tomorrow.*

*Dino is working at his desk when he hears a knock on his open office door. He looks up to see Hugo. Dino looks at Hugo and waits for him to speak.*

*'I'm confused,' Hugo says. The rest of their dialogue goes like this.*

DINO:    By what?

HUGO:    I appreciate your guidance in helping me adopt a broader perspective. I see the purpose, and I understand how it will help both me as a leader and the company's future. But now that I've taken on that broader perspective, I'm not sure how to be with those on my team.

DINO:    When you say you're not sure how to be with those on your team, what do you mean?

HUGO:    Well, they still look at things from a marketing perspective.

DINO:    As they should.

HUGO:    But I'm looking at things from a standpoint of overall value.

DINO:    As you should.

HUGO:    But the result is we're speaking different languages now.

DINO:    I hear what you're saying. You feel like you aren't looking out for them. Or that they feel you aren't looking out for them, because they see you with a different view all of a sudden. It's like you're abandoning the team.

HUGO:    Something like that.

DINO:    Well, the reality is, things are different now. You're straddling two worlds. You're still a member of that team, but you're also a member of this team. Not an easy spot to be in. The room is pretty different now when you walk in, isn't it?

HUGO:   Yes. They're much quieter around me. More cautious. Anxious, almost.

DINO:   It's a natural reaction on their part. They don't see you the same way anymore, because you don't occupy the same position anymore. You can't change that. They're going to be a lot more guarded around you now, because they see you as having information and power they don't have. So you have a separate challenge.

HUGO:   What's that?

DINO:   You need to be true to your new role and leverage the authority you've been given, while at the same time you need to manage this new dynamic. You're no longer their peer, Hugo. They know it and you know it. They're going to be careful around you, talk about you behind your back, keep things from you that they think might get them in trouble. It's a new world for you.

HUGO:   How do I manage it successfully?

DINO:   This conversation is a good start.

## Questions We Asked

1. How do you think Hugo should handle his new position with regard to his former peer group?
2. Have you ever been promoted to a new role and as a result struggled to know how to 'be' with your former peer group? Or have you ever, in general, walked into a room and people changed how they acted around how? How did it make you feel and how did you respond?
3. Have you ever been in a role where you felt like you had to straddle two different perspectives or outlooks? How did you manage this?

## Comments We Got

Everyone seems to recognize that Hugo is both a 'nice guy' and also rather on the timid side, so they have their concerns about his ability to both embrace his new authority as a general manager and also what people believe is the necessity for him to detach himself sufficiently from his former peers in order to be an effective leader to them.

Several of our participants reported personal experiences in which they struggled to strike this desired balance between staying 'plugged in' with those reporting to them while also establishing a clear leadership line. The majority told us that they have accomplished, or begun to accomplish, this goal by (a) maintaining strong consistency in their messaging and communication around a value orientation, (b) doing so always from an organizational view rather than a personal one, in order to avoid seeming as though it is 'their' message, and (c) ensuring the ongoing involvement and engagement of their team, but making sure to do so in the context of a shared focus and common goals. Most encourage Hugo to deliver a clear message to his team and, even more important, to show them, through the consistency and clarity of his behaviour, that he is a leader who can be counted on.

Our participants' overall responses centered around four different themes. Here they are, along with the most salient comments.

**1. Embrace, but don't abuse, the new role.**

'Hugo should lead some actions that will establish his authority, while avoiding undermining those who used to be his peers – a fine balance.'

'A company is made of human beings, with emotions. This doesn't make things easy.'

'Hugo needs to rebuild their trust. It is unsettling for his former peer group, so he needs to continue to work alongside them and tell them he will support their case while balancing the bigger picture. The most important thing early on is not to show his new position as one of power.'

'You just have to accept it. You feel lonely, but there is nothing you can do about it.'

## 2. Practice sensitivity and awareness.

'I think one caution that can't be overstated is that you really need to start watching what you say. Both from a "sharing confidential information" perspective and how your words are perceived and construed. If you were previously the first to respond to questions or offer input, you need to slow down now, as your word will be the final word on most matters. You also need to watch what you say about company leadership. Kicking the dog now needs to be done with peers, not your direct reports or your former peer group.'

'Attitude and behaviour is where we mostly fail. I would advise Hugo to be careful with both.'

## 3. Be a leader, but be open.

'He should also adapt his communication style, and content, with his team, taking into account his new position.'

'As a first-time people leader, I wasn't sure how "chummy" I should be. I found a balance by going out to lunch with my reports and others in my old peer group about once per month, while spending appropriate time with my "new" peer group.'

'Hugo should open up more and gain the confidence of his peers by asking for their support openly and providing them assistance voluntarily. He should seek to remove, block by block, the wall that his ex-peers will naturally start building around them from the moment he becomes their leader.'

'With my last move in the hierarchy, I had to learn that people start behaving differenly toward me, and that I don't get the same information/opinions from others I got before. My personal counter-measure: to go myself and see. I call on customers, I walk into the office of the person I want to talk to instead of calling them on the phone, I take people on my teams out for lunch. It isn't perfect, but it helps.'

'Hugo should convey that he will continue to help them and ask their support, but in a different way.'

**4. Act less like a boss and more like a company ambassador.**

'He needs to collaborate with them while aligning with the company vision.'

'I felt very lonely indeed, and tried to re-establish communication/collaboration with others on concrete actions, initiatives and projects, to build momentum around a common/shared purpose rather than around "me".'

'The role of the manager is to connect and channel efforts towards a common centre. We often need to adjust how we spell out requirements or expectations depending on to whom the message is being delivered, in order to achieve the common good for all.'

'As far as I can, I am trying to find the common tangible denominator to both perspectives. Hopefully one exists!'

'Although the perception from his former peers may be that he changed views, it is my experience that talking about the broader picture (as he just discovers it himself) should elevate the value of the whole team, as it will become easier to contribute to the company objectives with their team-lead now part of the executive team. Hugo should define the right balance on items he can share and topics he needs to keep confidential. Then decide on a compelling story line to keep his team connected. I do not have the experience that I was promoted over my peers.'

## Our Thoughts

Like Freddy and Nancy, Hugo is abruptly coming to realize that the relationship with his former peer group has changed. And, like Freddy and Nancy, he finds himself in an unfamiliar spot that requires him to both exercise leadership authority and manage a new, intricate, delicate dynamic.

Hugo's specific challenge is slightly different from that of Freddy or Nancy. Freddy, having increased his status in the eyes of senior management, must now pay close attention to the perceptions of those in his immediate circle and manage relationships effectively. Nancy, having taken up the mantle of value creation herself, must now think about how to communicate it to her team, through both her messages and behaviours. Hugo's test, at least as he puts it to Dino, is to continue to think and act from a perspective of value while still maintaining productive and candid relationships with those on the Marketing team from which he has come.

Though Hugo's precise circumstances somewhat contrast those of Freddy and Nancy, his overall challenge is the same: to espouse a clear, consistent message of value, to broadcast it unmistakably to the team, and to lead by example. He has accurately discovered that he must now toggle between multiple levels of the organization, that his role demands versatility and resourcefulness, and that nothing is as it was before. Even as he continues to discover new challenges, he seems to remain open to the journey ahead of him – a critical step. He is seeking guidance on how to navigate his new world, but he recognizes it as such, which positions him well to succeed.

**Your Thoughts**

\*   \*   \*

## Overall Discussion

In the previous chapter, each of our GMs came to recognize his or her new role as a facilitator of organizational value, instead of just a functional head. Now each of them has, in different ways, arrived at a new realization: that the way others see them has changed as well. Each of them encounters a situation that makes it clear to them they are no longer part of their former peer group, nor is it productive for them to try to be. It is different now. They must embrace their new circumstances and try to be the best leaders they can be in their new roles.

Furthermore, they recognize, when they encounter members of their former peer groups following their promotion, that the room is now different when they walk in. What was constant banter and an open exchange of information has been replaced by an odd kind of silence – which they may misinterpret as respect, or even admiration, but is more likely something like fear. What they must learn is that they need to undertake a complete shift of mentality in order to do their new job well. There are many ways in which their relationships have changed. No longer will people share information with them so freely. No longer will truthful statements be forthcoming. No longer will feedback be automatically believable or constructive. As our GMs come up again and again against situations that make clear they are no longer part of their former group, they must figure out how to leverage the new authority they've been given without destroying value within their own ranks.

How are they to do this? First, by establishing, and maintaining, a transparent dynamic and a constant flow of communication. Nothing can torpedo their leadership efforts more than an air of collective suspicion or secrecy among those on their teams. Their messages must be visible and obvious, so that others can easily emulate and reflect them. They must never appear to be pursuing a personal agenda or orchestrating things behind the scenes. They must strive to unambiguously confirm their position of leadership while still remaining connected to the team and sharing overall goals.

Second, it is crucial that they behave with absolute consistency, reinforcing over and over the messages they give to their teams. Those messages must be clear, concise and honest. It is of the utmost importance that they talk to everyone on the team the same way, communicate the same goals and focus on the same priorities. Coming from a group of peers and becoming leader to some of them, or all of them, is difficult. Different emotions can accompany the upward move and threaten one's chance for success – emotions like guilt, timidity, intimidation, embarrassment, insecurity and unease. As a result, a new GM may sometimes feel a pull back toward the space they occupied before, back to what they felt was comfortable, safe and familiar. Breaking out of an old role and stepping into a completely new one is far from easy. One method for easing the transition is to adopt simple messages and a straightforward style, so that those below them are always clear about what they expect and where their overall priorities lie.

Finally, and most important, they must lead by example. This means constantly putting their words into actions, living the messages they communicate, and making every decision based on a strict value orientation on behalf of the organization. There is no more effective way for our GMs to establish themselves in their new leadership roles than to *act* like leaders.

## Key Questions to Ask Yourself

1. Are you maintaining transparent and effective communication in all directions to ensure an ongoing perception of openness, honesty and fairness?

2. Are you being consistent in your messages and reinforcing consistent, coherent behaviours?
3. Are you leading by example by maintaining visible evidence of consistency between your words and behaviours, of your connection to the overall organization and of your commitment to long-term value creation?

# Chapter 5

# Bridging the Gap

## Freddy

### The Scenario

*A couple of days earlier, Freddy was summoned by Trish, his boss's boss, to discuss his growing profile, a direct result of his sound analysis of the potential Midwest toy company acquisition and senior management's decision to proceed based largely on the argument Freddy presented. Trish congratulated Freddy on his contribution, applauded his ability to go beyond an abstract argument and ground his analysis in data, and also issued him a word of warning regarding his new inadvertent position. With increased visibility, she told him, comes increased murmuring from others, and while his star may be rising with important decision-makers above, he should be aware that peers, direct reports and others around him may not be as enthusiastic. They will talk, she said. Some will be subtle, some more overt, but they will talk.*

*Freddy asked Trish how he should handle the new situation. She urged him to maintain his focus on the goal of long-term value for Prism, making decisions in support of that goal, and formulating arguments that try to explain the story he believes the data tells. There will be little he can do to influence the views of others, she said, besides continuing to see through this lens and communicating it consistently. His best hope will be for others to come around to the same perspective.*

*Vivian, Freddy's direct supervisor, is eating in the lunchroom when Freddy walks in. Freddy and Vivian have not yet discussed management's decision to pull the trigger on the toy company acquisition. Freddy has attempted a couple of times to find Vivian in her office or initiate a dialogue by e-mail, but each time he has come by, she has been away, and his e-mails have so far gone unacknowledged.*

*Here's how their conversation goes.*

FREDDY:  Hi, Vivian. How's your day going?

VIVIAN:  Oh, fine. Kudos on that analysis you did regarding the acquisition. I guess the powers that be really saw it your way.

FREDDY:  Well, I wouldn't say it's about who's right or wrong. I wasn't doing the analysis to contradict your view or win any argument. I was doing it to try to shed as much light as possible on the overall decision.

VIVIAN:  Still – you can't say you weren't leaning in a particular direction. I mean, the numbers you presented certainly supported the view you were asserting when we first had that meeting with Trish.

FREDDY:  I didn't manipulate any numbers.

VIVIAN:  I wouldn't suggest that. Maybe it's more accurate to say you conducted an analysis that supported a risky acquisition.

FREDDY:  You feel the acquisition was risky?

VIVIAN:  That's not what I said.

FREDDY:  Isn't that exactly what you just said?

VIVIAN:  Well, that's not what I meant. Your numbers suggested both investing in that new Chicago company and divesting our presence in areas where we've had a lot of success for a long time.

FREDDY:  Overall, the data argues for it.

VIVIAN:  It also argues for spending 12% more this year than our original budget.

FREDDY:  It highlights the position that a budget increase is justified if the investment is expected to yield a long-term positive return.

VIVIAN:    I just hope it works out. The board is practically ready to pull the plug on an entire market that we've been in for five decades.

FREDDY:    True, but that market is print media, and obviously people are spending more time online, and that trend isn't going to reverse. Our having been in anything for a long time doesn't necessarily justify continuing to be in it.

VIVIAN:    The new company only does digital media. What do we know about digital media?

FREDDY:    That's the point. We know a little, but part of the value of the acquisition is the knowledge we gain in return. The resulting combination should position us to make a strong play. It's a huge market and a big opportunity.

VIVIAN:    It takes time and effort to absorb new knowledge into the organization. In the meantime, we could go belly-up.

FREDDY:    According to the analysis, the resources we need to use to execute the transition won't prevent us from maintaining business as usual. In the meantime, if we miss the opportunity, it's sitting there for others to capture.

VIVIAN:    I just hope you're right.

FREDDY:    Well, again, I don't really care so much about whether I'm seen as right or not, and I'm not trying to do anything to have anybody say I'm right. I just think we should try to see things as clearly as possible, and the bigger the decision, the more informed our guess should be.

## Questions We Asked

1. Why do you think Vivian is displaying such resistance/resentment toward Freddy? What do you think he should do about it?

2. Freddy reports to Vivian. Should he acquiesce to her opinions or stick to what he believes is right for the company?

3. Have you ever had to deal with a strong reaction from a colleague or supervisor who felt you were getting recognized or rewarded for a view with which he or she disagreed?

## Comments We Got

Our participants had a lot to say about the fraught-with-tension conversation between Freddy and Vivian. They felt that Freddy was ambushed by Vivian's passive-aggressiveness, but that he handled himself pretty well, staying composed and speaking to the data instead of letting emotions or personal opinion get in the way.

At the same time, many people offered words of caution for Freddy to heed. While almost everyone seemed to feel that his value orientation is correct, they also pointed out that he needs to be extra careful at this point, since Vivian seems to feel threatened or resentful toward him, and he did, after all, submit the analysis to Trish without consulting Vivian or seeking her opinion on it. The general consensus was that, while Freddy is doing a good job of explaining his position after the fact, he would have benefited from considering in advance how his boss might react.

Five major themes came out of our participants' overall responses. Here they are, with representative comments included.

**1. If you can support it with data and logic, argue for it ...**

'Freddy should stick to what he believes is right for the company.'

'Freddy needs to go at this patiently and persistently. It takes time to lobby and educate on the right goals for the company.'

**2. ... but be mindful of how you go about it ...**

'It is obvious that Freddy's thought process and decision-making did not involve his hierarchy, who would be directly impacted by the change. Resistance within and "above" the team might undermine the success of the resulting implementation.'

'In this case, the subordinate has been given an opportunity to present his view, contradictory to his boss. Freddy knew Vivian had a different view before presenting. I think he should have warned her of his intention, since nobody likes to be surprised.

She could have tried to change his mind, but this also could have been a great opportunity for him to defend and explain his case better up front. This can be a dangerous game to play, and it certainly does not help trust.'

'Vivian has a different perspective; and maybe she has been part of the decisions about the corporate strategy in previous times. So even when Freddy is right, she might feel it as an attack on what she has been doing. Freddy should try to communicate himself to Vivian as effectively as possible, explaining why he believes his rationale is correct.'

'Freddy's arguments/views are based on opinions which do not align with Vivian's. She appears to be risk-averse, while he appears to be quite inclined toward innovation. To try to lower her resistance/resentment toward him, Freddy should perhaps further detail how his recommendation for change/innovation is not in contradiction of Vivian's opinion, but rather supports a natural evolution of the market – and that if this is not addressed, the sustainability of the business will be jeopardized. Freddy should detail, in a rational and factual way, the reason it is time for change.'

'Freddy should definitely stick to his views, so long as he has the necessary facts. At the same time, he needs to respect his supervisor – to an extent – and acknowledge her views. It does appear he has gone about this without her support or backing, which is very risky.'

'Vivian has a strong bias toward investing in the traditional businesses in the company. She might also have been looking forward to getting resources that were directed at the newer investments. Freddy might suggest spending some more time with her to see if she has issues with, or differing views on, some of the data points underlying his recommended strategy. It could be that more time with the data will change her opinion toward it.'

'I would not play it like Freddy did.'

**3. ... and be diplomatic about taking credit.**

'A couple of times when I was in Technical Service, I was in conflict with people in R&D who were the 'owners' of technology.
When I proposed an idea, I was shot down and told I didn't
know the science. Then we tried it and it worked, and then I
was told the data was fabricated because it couldn't possibly
work. Then I was recognized, and the attacks were frequent
and harsh. I finally spent some time going over the data and
came up with a way for the R&D guys to save face around
the data, and I shared some of the recognition with them (i.e.
"Look at what we came up with!"). A bit painful for me, but
I realized that allowing them to save face at the "expense" of
my own recognition was more productive and better for our
needed working relationship going forward!'

'My take is that Vivian is upset simply because one of her subordinates got heard by her bosses. How does it feel when one of
your people defends an idea which is not yours and receives
positive feedback from your boss?'

'Vivian feels overruled. Freddy made a recommendation without including her and, even worse, one that was contrary to
what she would have recommended. Freddy needs to do some
damage control. He should calm things down by saying there
are two views, the data support A or B, or both, depending
on your assumptions and long-term view of the markets. They
should prepare a joint memo emphasizing the different views
and ways to come to a risk-based consensus approach, then
ask for an open brainstorm session with higher management,
who need to hear the full argument – not the only the opinion
of the one who spoke first.'

'Vivian is averse to drastic change; she hopes the traditional business can turn around with some adjustment, but her own staff
is proposing the opposite approach. More important, Freddy's
analysis is being appreciated by upper management. The difference in their opinions is one thing, but it seems she may

be envious of, or threatened by, his success in these circumstances.'

'Freddy has to stick to what seems to be a well-supported opinion
and engage Vivian so she can get on the same wavelength and
share the credit.'

## 4. Keep opinions out of it, always.

'He needs to get Vivian on board. It will be extremely difficult
to overcome her opposition. The challenge is to convince her
with facts, not opinions.'

'Freddy should stick to what he believes is right for the company,
so long as he can support his argument with comprehensive
research and opinion-free analysis.'

'I believe you need to stick with what you believe in, but it is
important to base it on facts, not gut.'

'Since Vivian disagrees with Freddy's view on the required strategy, it would help for him to engage with her – earlier in the
process if possible – and seek her buy-in. He should use fact,
not opinion, to support his arguments.'

## 5. Even when you think you're right, others can still be helpful.

'Freddy should stick to what he believes is right. But it could be
that Vivian has a perspective which could shed light on the
decision that he and the others haven't considered.'

'Vivian has experience in the field, and her knowledge and part-
nership can also serve Freddy well here.'

'Of course Freddy should stick to what he believes is right for the
company, but he has to try to reason from the perspectives of
Vivian and others. Maybe she is also right, in a different way –
or it may help him to explain his vision from her perspective.'

## Our Thoughts

In questioning the company's traditional ways of doing things
and pushing for an objective consideration of the new investment,

Freddy has done the right thing for the organization. In sidestepping Vivian, he has committed a not-insignificant blunder, which he now must address head-on. Vivian is still his boss, and the boss has a right to expect transparency, full disclosure in all things and, most important, an expectation that everyone is playing for the team. While Freddy's idea is absolutely team-oriented in the broadest sense – that is, his overall purpose is to ensure long-term health for Prism – he has misstepped when it comes to his immediate political environment.

Whether Vivian agrees with his view is less important than the manner in which Freddy has gone about this behaviour. Vivian's risk-averse attitude is as obvious as Trish's similarly conservative one. But Trish has allowed and encouraged Freddy to pursue his concern that the company may not be making decisions for the right reasons, whereas Vivian seems much more loath to any kind of change in approach or attitude. Freddy's emphatic intuition that innovation is necessary for the company is admirable. It can only help Prism in the long run. But going above your supervisor is risky business.

Freddy most likely did not do this intentionally. In getting Trish's permission to conduct the analysis, he probably didn't think of it as doing an end-around on Vivian. But their conversation in the lunchroom seems to imply that Vivian sees it exactly this way. Even though Freddy is doing his best to try to deny Vivian's not-so-subtle accusations that he is in it for personal gain, he is clearly on the defensive and unsure how to respond.

At this point, he has no choice but to stay on course – to make sure Vivian knows, or hopefully comes to accept, that his only aim in performing the analysis was to assess the long-term value for the company, and in so doing perhaps begin to highlight a new way of looking at potential investments in the future. Vivian may continue to resist this assertion, and the resentment she is displaying toward Freddy may not go away quickly.

Freddy's best move is to alter his political approach, starting immediately. Without compromising his overall value orientation, it is essential that he become more conscious of involving Vivian in 'upward' decisions from now on. He will have to slowly try to chip away at both Vivian's resistance to change as well as her umbrage toward him that has unfortunately now taken root. The way for him to do this will be to continue to argue from a point of view of data, but to engage her earlier in the process, to ask for – and integrate – her contribution and to then present recommendations that don't seem individually motivated. Freddy's commitment to value and his willingness to stick his neck out have put him in a favourable position with those at the top levels of the company strata, but he needs to become more conscious of the fact that a pecking order still exists, and that, if he ruffles the wrong feathers, he may find himself in an untenable position regardless of how those at the top of the ladder see him.

**Your Thoughts**

# Nancy

## The Scenario

*In her previous conversation with Calvin, Nancy cited a dilemma that she herself was surprised by. She was coming to find that in conversations with her own team, she would echo Dana's perspective on long-term vision and true value drivers rather than focusing on KPIs and short-term targets like she had been accustomed to doing. Calvin congratulated Nancy for this, telling her it represented a positive broadening of her viewpoint.*

*That wasn't all, Nancy said. The more pressing matter was that she now felt deficient in communicating with her direct reports, and that she suddenly represented something, and someone, different to them. She was concerned that they were no longer relating to her on either a personal or business level.*

*Calvin said he understood, and encouraged Nancy to try to make her team think from the same value perspective as she herself was coming around to. They are used to focusing on hitting their targets, earning their bonuses and striving for promotions, he said, so it's startling for them to hear a different viewpoint. He advised Nancy not to try to explode their ideas overnight but instead to take their current style of thinking about targets and KPIs and try to fit them into a bigger discussion of sustainable value and what it means for Tipton. Finally, Calvin told Nancy, it is imperative that she lead by example, and that consistency between her message and her behaviour will be vital to her team's buy-in.*

*The next afternoon, Nancy is pouring herself a cup of coffee at the office kitchenette when Dana walks in. The following exchange ensues.*

DANA:     Afternoon.
NANCY:   Hi, Dana. How are you?
DANA:     Fine, thanks. And you?
NANCY:   Can't complain.

| | |
|---|---|
| DANA: | Hey, listen, if you wanted to take some time for me to explain further what I was talking about in the meeting with Calvin, I'd be happy to. |
| NANCY: | What's that? |
| DANA: | He told me you were starting to come over to my side regarding the value discussion. |
| NANCY: | Your side? |
| DANA: | Yes – he said you told him you were starting to see the value concept more the way I was trying to explain it when we were in his office. As opposed to your focus on targets and KPIs. It's so hard to have that epiphany sometimes, but when you have it, it's great, because it can lead to so much more learning. Anyway, any time you'd like to talk further about, I can get into more details. It's one of those topics for me. |
| NANCY: | One of those topics … |
| DANA: | Everyone has stuff they know really well and stuff they don't. This is just one of those areas I understand really well. I think it can take time to get. I'm sure at your old company there was probably a big emphasis on targets and other traditional metrics. It's probably really hard to let go of that mentality, right? |
| NANCY: | I'm not sure. I still think targets and KPIs are very important. |
| DANA: | Yes, yes, they are. I mean, as part of the larger picture of value. |
| NANCY: | You certainly make it sound simple. |
| DANA: | No, I don't think it's simple at all. That's why I'm offering to help you with it, if you'd like. I struggled with the idea at first, too. |
| NANCY: | Perhaps both sides of the argument have validity. |
| DANA: | I would challenge that assumption. I think there is actually only one valid perspective, which is a long-term value orientation. |
| NANCY: | And you're saying there's no place for traditional metrics in that orientation. |
| DANA: | No, I'm not saying that. I feel like you aren't hearing me clearly, or it may just be tough for you to get your head around it. I mean, it definitely takes more than one conversation. Are you sure you wouldn't like to spend some time going through it together? |
| NANCY: | Why don't I see what my calendar is like and get back to you? |
| DANA: | Perfect. Let me know. |

## Questions We Asked

1. How would you feel in Nancy's position coming out of this conversation with Dana?
2. If you were in Nancy's position, would you accept Dana's offer to discuss the concept further?
3. Have you ever had a colleague who felt it would benefit you to see things 'their' way? How did you manage the situation?

## Comments We Got

Dana is no less than a polarizing figure, eliciting ire from some of our contributors, shock from others, sympathy from a handful. A number of people said that, in Nancy's spot, they would want nothing at all to do with this 'colleague' and would make every attempt to sever the relationship with her, at least to the extent possible within the broader context of the team. Others took a cooler view, asserting that, despite Dana's disagreeable ways, it is still of the utmost importance for Nancy to maintain a positive rapport with her, since contributing to a negative dynamic can only harm the long-term prognosis for both her and the organization.

Dana's behaviour was not debated; everyone found it at the least unpleasant, at the worst atrocious. To some, the stoic approach seemed most useful for Nancy – let Dana say what she has to say, and then move on and get things done, hoping she won't run constant interference. Others disagreed, believing that a person like Dana must be either confronted, acquiesced to or subtly brought onside. As a general trend, the more senior of those among our participant community seemed to be most in favour of a 'soft' strategy with Dana: accept her invitation, attempt to engage in a professional discussion about the topic at hand and, as distasteful as the prospect may seem, embrace the relationship as a necessary one to be diligently managed instead of as a destructive one to be tirelessly avoided.

The overall responses we received revolved around four recognizable themes. Here they are, along with some of the more notable comments.

**1. Certain colleagues can be hard to deal with ...**

'I would be considering the ways that I could inflict slow, painful torture on Dana. Maybe find ways to sneak powdered capsicum into her tea?'

'I would feel that Dana is continuously undermining my view and position and that she has a single objective to "move me to her side" with no room for seeing/doing things "my way".'

'With Dana, I would listen politely, as Nancy does. What else can you do with someone like that?'

'I would not want to talk to Dana again. Even if I know this may not be a good idea politically, I would still stay away from her as much as possible.'

'Dana's patronizing tone, sneaky approach and awkward timing for such a conversation should make Nancy think twice on her real motives. If long-term value is what Dana is after, she certainly started on the wrong path by shining the spotlight all on herself.'

'If I were Nancy, I would feel pretty annoyed not so much by the fact that Dana has a different opinion, but more by her approach and style.'

'Dana's tone makes me feel from the start that she has a hidden agenda, and she makes me feel that she does not respect or acknowledge Nancy's background, experience or vision. She clearly views Nancy as inferior, and this does not create trust.'

'Coming out of this conversation, I would be puzzled how to handle Dana!'

**2. ... but they still might be worth listening to.**

'As insulting as Dana was, I would give her the benefit of the doubt. She may have some stories or examples from her history that would help me understand the ideas a little better. I would also prepare for the meeting to help her understand that there are still purposes for tracking measurements (primarily to facilitate business understanding). I would try to come up with some good questions for her to answer.'

'As hard as it would be for me to do it, I would try to hear Dana out – as long as the tone of the discussion is fair.'

'As challenging as Dana is, one can learn from these exchanges, and also find out more about where they stand. I'd like to find out more about why Dana believes that she is the one with a clear understanding. Knowing what the other person believes and how she argues for it can be beneficial to determining a personal strategy or vision.'

'Dana's approach is terrible, and I don't think it would be easy for me to control my emotions with her – but the point has to be to find the best strategy for the company in the end. If it is the right idea, it doesn't matter "whose way" it is.'

'I had a serious difference of opinion with a colleague a while back. It caused a severe clash, and the other party ended up moving on. Looking back on it, I think there might have been some value in what she was bringing to the table, but I was perhaps too junior still to be able to distinguish content (there is almost always something of use to derive) from form (I felt intimidated, and therefore defensive).'

'I think it's always important to try to understand someone else's perspective. For instance, in this case, Nancy should seek to understand why Dana is so insistent that there is only one valid perspective. What in her background would make her so opposed to short-term measures? Why is it that everyone needs to align with her beliefs and opinions? I would also ask for Dana's background from her colleagues to try to understand her a little more, since understanding the events or situations in a person's past is always valuable. I also tend to think that it's not harmful to be agreeable with people on points that really don't matter in the grand scheme of things.'

3. **Stay professional. Always seek to turn adversaries into collaborators.**

'Early in my career, I would not have been interested at all to talk to Dana further. Now, I might call her in and try to help her see better ways to get things done.'

'Generally, it makes sense to listen to others, as you almost always will find something of their opinion of use. With Dana, the key point is tone and style. I would struggle with Dana's approach, and it would take some effort on my part to hold back.'

'I would give Dana the opportunity to convert me to a different opinion, or to confirm the validity of the opinion I already have. I am unsure, given Dana's behaviour, that I would try to convince her, though.'

'I personally would accept Dana's offer – to show I'm above her petty behaviour.'

'When I have a colleague who insists on "their" way, I try to listen to them to understand what constitutes the ground of our differing perspectives, and then assess my own interest in moving 'their way' or retaining my position. That's how I would deal with Dana in this situation.'

'I would absolutely accept Dana's offer, and I would make sure it is done as soon as possible so that I would have the opportunity to get my point of view clear and clarify in my own words what I agree with and what I am not yet convinced of. I would try to keep the discussion objective and avoid any attempts at personal commentary. I would also fight any 'patronizing' tone by intercepting the discussion at any point I feel such tone is being used. Go for it, Nancy!'

4. **Keep your adversaries close.**

'I suppose it's possible I might learn from Dana's point of view, but most likely she is a conscious hurdle for me. If that's the case, there is all the reason in the world not to keep too much distance from her.'

## Our Thoughts

To someone as consciously self-possessed as Nancy, Dana must seem like a Doberman always ready to strike. After this kind of conversation, the strong inclination for an individual like Nancy will no doubt be to avoid all further contact with Dana. We can only imagine that Nancy is ready to throw her hands up and wonder if there is any way she can turn this relationship positive. Likely coming up with no good answer, it is a near certainty that every instinct in Nancy's body is telling her to just steer clear of Dana, cultivate the more productive relationship with Calvin, and hope for the best.

But to do so would be a grave mistake. As much as she would probably like to, Nancy cannot snap her fingers and magically make Dana disappear. Nancy ought to instead look at Dana for what she is: someone whose style contrasts with her own. And, as many of you pointed out, someone she can potentially learn from. Nancy is unaccustomed to Dana's aggressive manner and it has her on her heels, feeling like she wants, more than anything else, to just retreat. Once Nancy's initial shock wears off, she needs to try to change her perception of the relationship with Dana. Though her delivery may not exactly be admirable, Dana is nonetheless someone with knowledge, expertise and, at bottom, a perspective which is not the same as Nancy's.

Nancy should regard this as an opportunity, instead of the sinkhole she may currently view it as. If Dana really does have such a good grasp on value creation and ways in which short-term targets and KPIs can be used to foster that overall goal, then she can be a valuable resource to Nancy as she warms up to this new way of thinking. Recall that Nancy herself is making a transition in her thinking about the role of KPIs in managing her team. Her team has not yet made this transition and, most likely, Nancy is not yet in a position of mastering her own understanding to be able to competently engage her team on the subject. In other words, she could use the help, and as much as Dana's style is off-putting, she is still a potential source of knowledge and perspective on a topic relatively new to Nancy's way of thinking. Nancy should recognize that her own reluctance is due to a natural but counterproductive emotional response to Dana's style.

Naturally, engaging with someone like Dana may be difficult for someone like Nancy. She needs to see the relationship as one that will take time to find its stride and its rhythm, but which has a chance to be mutually constructive in the long run. For Nancy, making a concerted attempt to connect with Dana will also send the right message to Calvin. Dana has reached out to Nancy and offered help, even if Nancy may not like the way the offer was presented. Avoiding Dana or rejecting her olive branch would put Nancy in a dangerous position, given the perception of resistance or aversion she may convey to Calvin.

Dana is not the only peer, boss or subordinate whose style will be different from the type Nancy is used to, or most comfortable with. To carry out her new managerial role successfully, she cannot just ignore or avoid situations that require direct engagement with others. A leader must be willing to engage in the tough conversations and find a way to extract the positive from challenging circumstances. It is an example Nancy needs to show not only to her team, but also to herself.

**Your Thoughts**

# Hugo

## The Scenario

*In their conversation a few days earlier, Hugo came to Dino asking for help. Hugo, ever the willing student, had accepted the need to move from a functional view to one of value creation, but when interacting with the former marketing peers now reporting to him, he found it was difficult to speak the same language or find a point of connection. Dino advised him that he was now straddling two worlds, the old one in which he was a marketing expert, and the new one in which his role is to contribute to decisions that will produce value for AMR in the long term. Dino told him it is a new part of his learning curve. There is the numbers part, and there is the people part.*

*Dino has e-mailed Hugo requesting a meeting with himself and Peter Falkenberg, VP Asia, whom Hugo encountered briefly at his first meeting with the senior executive team, but with whom he has not yet interacted directly. When Hugo enters, Dino and Peter are already seated. Here's how the meeting goes:*

DINO:   Good morning, Hugo. Come on in. You remember Peter from the executive meeting.

PETER:  How's it going?

        *(Peter raises his fist for a fist-bump from Hugo. Hugo pauses, then hesitantly fist-bumps Peter, who gives him a friendly but firm slap on the shoulder.)*

DINO:   You two are counterparts – Hugo for EMEA, Peter for Asia. Hugo, Peter comes from a hardware background.

HUGO:   Computer hardware?

PETER:  No – real hardware. Wrenches, screwdrivers, saws, ratchets … nuts-and-bolts stuff. Now I'm working for a company that makes fuzzy dolls for kids! They must have hired me for my looks.

DINO:   You met in passing at the exec meeting, and I just wanted us to spend a bit more time talking about where we are so that we're on the same page going forward.

PETER:  *(to Hugo, with a grin)* Actually, I think he hired us both so he could have a little more testosterone in those exec meetings.

HUGO:  Uh …

DINO:  Listen, I want to have a conference sometime within the next two months for your combined staff. We're going to present the key initiatives that are going to be rolled out next year. I want you two to lead it.

PETER:  Sounds awesome.

*(Peter holds up his fist to Hugo again. Hugo tentatively gives him another fist-bump.)*

DINO:  I'm going to e-mail you some broad-stroke details about the initiatives to give you the right amount of baseline information, then I'd like the two of you to draft an agenda. I'd like to be able to look at it by the end of next week.

PETER:  You want to have a successful conference? Spend as little time as possible talking about the initiatives.

HUGO:  I beg your pardon?

PETER:  People hate that crap. It takes about two minutes before they want to get out of there and go for a swim in the hotel pool or go to their room and watch a movie. You want to know what motivates people at a conference? Having fun. What you do is some of those icebreaker games, trust exercises, all that stuff. Celebrate birthdays, company anniversaries. They eat it up. And they feel like a team when they leave. Honestly, how long does it take to explain an initiative? You tell them this is what we're doing, go do it – Now let's have a jigsaw puzzle contest!

HUGO:  Well, but you also need to make sure they understand the purpose of the initiatives, the mechanisms and the objectives. If they don't, execution will be sub-optimal.

PETER:  *Sub-optimal* – I love it. Dude, you sound like you're reading from a textbook! Of course they need to know why and how. But again, these people aren't morons. Well, maybe some of them are morons …

HUGO:  Um …

DINO:    Why don't you both review the e-mail and then book time in my calendar to discuss the agenda? After that, we can talk about further details. Okay?

HUGO:    Sure.

PETER:   Aces! *(to Hugo)* Talk at ya later.

## Questions We Asked

1. Hugo and Peter are clearly different. How do you think Hugo should manage this new relationship?
2. Have you ever had a counterpart who was very different from you? How did you handle it?
3. Who do you think is better at his job, Hugo or Peter? Why?

## Comments We Got

Our participants were amused by Peter's blustery, not-at-all-by-the-book behaviour, but also concerned with respect to how Hugo might handle, or not handle, this new relationship. People recognized the obvious differences in the approaches and dispositions of the two foils, and offered numerous suggestions as to ways in which Hugo might seek to maximize his association with Peter instead of avoiding it – which might certainly be his instinct given his seeming shyness and naturally low-key manner.

Many encouraged Hugo to look past Peter's veneer and seek the expert beneath, who, after all, must have earned his position as GM Asia for worthwhile reasons. In every company, people noted, there are a great variety of personalities and attitudes, and the sooner you stop hoping that everyone else will behave the same as yourself, the better chance you have at nurturing fruitful relationships and performing successfully in your role. Our participants' general advice to Hugo was to maintain composure, try to spend time with Peter, focus on the business instead of the superficial behaviours, and find ways in which the differences between the two could be turned into value for AMR.

Three particular themes emerged from the overall reactions to the meeting among Dino, Hugo and Peter. Here they are, accompanied by some of the more salient individual comments received.

## 1. Turn contrasts into opportunities.

'These two need to work together, so the initiative of getting them working on a joint assignment is a good one. Clearly some give-and-take will need to happen if they are to be successful.'

'Hugo should spend more time with Peter to observe his performance, thought process and communication style. At the same time, it is an opportunity for Hugo to let Peter understand him.'

'Hugo and Peter should recognize that there is an opportunity here to combine strengths and achieve an even greater whole than the sum of its parts. Plus, their boss wants them to work together, so they better figure out how to do it, even if it may be difficult due to their very different personalities. They should focus on the work to be done, not the differences in who they are.'

'You have to assume these two have been employed for the complementary skills they bring, so it's important that they try to get the best out of each other.'

'I've really had to adjust my behavioural adaptation to circumstances like the one Hugo is facing. I have traditionally not fared well when encountering colleagues who are very different to me. After a lot of help and training, I am now better aware of how others perceive me. I used to miss it completely. Now I am able to use it to our mutual advantage.'

'I think Hugo is in shock! We might have a case of an extreme extravert versus introvert. Hugo will need to step up and get to know Peter. He should also take the initiative to initiate the meeting with Peter to get to know him better and then tackle the topic/agenda at hand.'

'If I were Hugo, I would make a point of openly acknowledging the differences, and then focusing on the common goal – and understanding together that there are different ways to achieve it.'

'Hugo and Peter obviously have nothing in common. Peter's fist-bump, the pat on the back, the permanent smile – all are body language that obviously make Hugo uncomfortable. But Peter is as vulnerable as Hugo is, and I believe their differences are only superficial. I think their differences could be seen as complementary styles, and that is what they should seek to take advantage of. There are things Hugo can do to work effectively with Peter, like asking closed questions to keep him contained and taking back possession of the discussion at timely moments in order to stop Peter's flow. Hugo should also resist being influenced by the assertive tone in Peter's statements and suggestions.'

'The best outcome will result if Dino manages the relationship between Hugo and Peter effectively, so that both can contribute to a common strategy. It is out of such diversity that companies can draw strength. Too many of one type or the other would not be good, but the balance between these two might work very well.'

'Peter just strikes me as a guy who is a little too wild, and his self-confidence seems a bit misplaced. However, there's a good chance that Hugo will be able to learn from him – things like out-of-the-box thinking, his background in "real" hardware, his thoughts on people leading and ways to do team building, etc. There is always room for multiple perspectives. This could be the reason why Dino hired Peter in the first place.'

'Peter lacks experience and needs coaching. He seems extremely vocal, sharing his opinions without seeming to consider them for too long. At least you know where he stands, though a little reflection might benefit him. Hugo appears more serious and professional in his gestures and choice of words, but he needs to speak up more and be firmer in his opinions. I think the two can learn a lot from each other, and each can bring out something new in the other, to the overall benefit of the organization.'

## 2. Judge the book by the content, not the cover.

'Peter is a big contrast to Hugo, but I think it would be a potential pitfall for Hugo to decide that he doesn't like Peter just because he is so different from him. Hugo should try to keep an open mind when working with Peter, and to create space to share his own ideas so they can build up respect for each other's way of working. The only thing that matters is whether Peter is good at what he does.'

'Hugo should challenge Peter's opinions and assertions in a friendly, collaborative way, to show that he is genuinely interested in Peter's position, but that he needs Peter to explain and justify his opinions.'

'Colleagues often have contrasting personalities, styles or approaches. It's always important to listen to the other person try to understand their point of view. Everyone has something to give.'

## 3. Seek common ground.

'Hugo needs to get to know Peter, and the two of them together must find a common point of interest and focus. At times it seems almost impossible to find commonality, but it's important to make your best effort to do so.'

'I had a colleague whose style and approach were very different from mine, and I didn't handle it very well. I was always trying to convince the other party that my way was the right way. Finally I learned to be collaborative instead of insisting on my way, and we then learned to appreciate each other's strengths.'

'I encountered a situation like this, with a colleague whose manner was very different from mine, and I handled it poorly. The colleague and I ended up always either in confrontation or no communication at all. I regret to say I never found the way for us to come together.'

## Our Thoughts

As a number of you pointed out, there is only one relevant factor for Hugo to focus on: Peter's strengths as a manager. He should do everything in his power to resist being distracted by the difference between Peter's behaviour and his own. That said, it is of course easy to advise someone not to be distracted by personality and behaviour. It is less easy to do. And the contrast between Hugo and Peter is not small. Peter is, as noted frequently in our contributors' comments, an extreme extravert if there ever was one, prone to quick statements and strong, often blanket, opinions. Hugo's style, on the other hand, is the virtual opposite: reserved, unhurried, inquisitive, exploring. You could easily imagine how the interpretation of these differences could be magnified if Peter and Hugo came from different national cultures.

Hugo's situation is somewhat similar to the one Nancy finds herself in, but also different in an important way. Whereas both GMs have encountered peers whose styles conflict dramatically with their own, Nancy's situation carries with it, at least to her perception, a tone of antagonism. Hugo's feeling toward Peter is more likely one of shock than hostility. During the three-way discussion in which Dino assigned Hugo and Peter joint responsibility for planning the upcoming conference involving both their staff, Hugo was like a deer in the headlights in response to his new colleague's unfiltered, vocal, slightly chauvinistic attitude and 'big' personality. We can assume he walked out of Dino's office feeling like a tornado had just passed through.

The trick for Hugo will be to manage his initial reaction of shock and not allow it to morph unfairly – and unproductively – into dislike or avoidance of Peter. Though he may not recognize it at first, Hugo has a major opportunity here. He and Peter in all likelihood have complementary talents, and the personality and style of each can probably benefit the other. Peter may be able to bring Hugo out of his shell a bit, and Hugo may be able to ground Peter, to their reciprocal benefit and to the advantage of the organization.

With Hugo GM for EMEA and Peter GM for Asia, there will be regular interaction between the two, as they reside at the same level of the company org chart, and both report to Dino. Hugo has been with AMR for 14 years; it is the only company he has worked for since graduating with his MBA degree. Peter, on the other hand, has joined the company only recently, after spending time in a very different environment. This, too, is a factor that Hugo should do his best to leverage. Peter brings to the management level at AMR a diverse background Hugo himself cannot claim. It is in Hugo's absolute interests to get to know his new colleague well, seek common ground, and adopt the attitude that each can help get the best out of the other.

**Your Thoughts**

\* \* \*

## Overall Discussion

Each of our three GMs, having discovered that they must change their mentality regarding the definition and management of value, now face a different realization: their new roles also demand a serious change in the way they deal with people. The managerial positions into which they have stepped, while granting them greater authority and responsibility, also make them more vulnerable, and any of their potential missteps are more exposed. They are now managing multiple dynamics at once – those with bosses, those with peers and those with subordinates. Before, at a more junior level and as part of a less visible team, they had the partial luxury of flying under the radar. This luxury no longer exists. They must enhance their own radar and be constantly sensitive to every relationship, while maintaining focus on the business and the overall goal of creating long-term value for their respective firms.

All three GMs in addition must increase their emotional intelligence in two specific areas. First, they need to increase their self-awareness – that is, their ability to understand themselves and how others see them. Nancy may have been put off by what she perceived as Dana's aggressiveness, but what does Nancy know about how Dana perceives her behaviour? We sometimes spend so much effort on our emotional responses to others' behaviours that we forget our own ways also trigger emotions in others. Second, our GMs need to increase their ability to *mentalize* – that is, their ability to set aside their initial emotional response to someone's behaviours and instead put themselves on the balcony to observe the bigger picture. Why might Dana or Peter behave the way they do? The more our GMs make the effort to understand that there are many explanations for any person's actions, the more they may become curious to find out more about that person instead of focusing on their own emotional responses.

The need to manage these relationships isn't about internal politics. As we have emphasized, one of the primary functions of the GM role is to maintain team morale and enthusiasm in all directions – below, above and laterally. Another assertion we have made is the need to recognize that the GM sphere is large and highly complex, and thus the successful GM continuously seeks new insights, new information and new perspectives from which to build an integrated and long-term view. This requires finding ways to communicate and work with people of different backgrounds and lenses. Often it is those who are the most 'different' who can add the most value. This is the value of diversity – diversity of education, diversity of functional and industry experience, diversity of cultural experience and background, diversity of knowledge and perspective – that is critical to ensure the GM maintains his or her ability to continuously learn about, and incorporate, the broad perspective needed to manage for value.

Senior leaders in any organization must abandon their leaning toward any one perspective in order to make decisions based on an overall, inclusive value standpoint, whether the contrast is represented by hard business expertise, experiential knowledge or personal style. Freddy, for example, started by arguing for innovation and value creation, but found that his arguments fell on deaf ears. Nancy, stuck in a particular way of thinking about targets and KPIs, struggled to see the forest for the trees – the trees representing the hard indicators she had become accustomed to managing, the forest a broader notion of value. Hugo entered his first executive meeting eager to present marketing's perspective, only to be told by his boss that it was the last thing he should be doing.

Now, each of our GMs has discovered that, to achieve success and build value, they must find a way to manage the people part of their new role as much as the business part. Freddy has quickly come to learn that he must balance his vigilant focus on long-term value creation against the agendas of Vivian and Trish, as well as the potential resentments of those below him. Nancy seems to have at least partially embraced the logic of the value argument – instead of managing the indicators directly, she has come to understand that it is crucial to manage the underlying drivers of value, even if they are often harder to discern – but her main issue is now in dealing with a colleague who ruffles her feathers. Hugo started by understanding that the hazard of building expertise in one area is the inability to see things from contrasting points of view, and he has evolved from that perspective, placing aside his years of functional training and discarding his own ideas and opinions in order to understand value in a more sophisticated way. However, he is struggling to learn how to communicate in different ways with the different groups to which he is now connected, including the marketing group that now reports to him, his boss Dino and his blunt, outspoken counterpart Peter.

What all three GMs are discovering is that an essential part of their potential success as general managers will involve how effectively they can manage the various personalities, sensibilities and approaches of those around them. They can no longer afford to view things from only one perspective, or in just one way. They must strive to create an open, trusting environment in which crucial information is freely shared, honest feedback routinely given, and the overall aim of value creation pursued collectively. To do this, they must establish rapport with different people, which requires a delicate, informed balancing act. Their peers, their reports and their superiors represent different backgrounds, cultures and personalities, and thus diverse ways of seeing things and making decisions, and they must be aware of, and responsive to, each and every one of these.

Everyone operates differently based on where, and what, they have come from. To thrive in their GM roles, Freddy, Nancy and Hugo must understand these different perspectives and respond to them astutely. If they are to promote an environment in which the long-term health and success of the organization is the one true goal, they must exercise patience; they must resist jumping to conclusions; they must acknowledge that others' actions and behaviours may not necessarily mirror their own; and they must, above all, place any judgements aside in deference to objectively asking the question, 'Does this create value?' and ensuring those around them commit to doing the same.

## Key Questions to Ask Yourself

1. Are you cognizant of the political positioning of those around you and how your own views fit in with theirs?
2. How effectively are you able to separate the substantive issues from the personal/political issues in your work relationships? Are you able to remain constructive and learning-oriented in the face of difficult colleagues or unpleasant relationships?
3. It is extremely difficult to withhold judgement of, and maintain respect for, colleagues whose behaviours, styles or viewpoints are different from our own. Do you consciously strive to seek out, and work effectively with, those whose styles and views contrast your own in order to maximize your learning? Are you able to communicate and build relationships successfully in spite of these differences?

# Chapter 6

---

# Walking the Talk

## Freddy

### The Scenario

*A few days earlier, Freddy had a tense lunchroom interaction with his boss, Vivian, about his analysis of the potential Midwest toy company acquisition, which is now going ahead. Vivian faux-congratulated him on his contribution to the decision, but then passive-aggressively accused him of manipulating the argument to support a view he already held.*

*Freddy countered by saying that he had not conducted the analysis with any particular conclusion in mind, but that he was simply trying to look through a value-creation lens and make a recommendation that would support Prism's long-term sustainability. Vivian re-asserted her opinion that the acquisition is risky for a number of reasons, including divesting assets in areas where the company has been a player for decades and increasing short-term expenditures for uncertain future return. Following the advice of Trish, Freddy did his best to talk only about the story he believes the data was telling – that the acquiring company's experience in digital media will contribute to true value, that Prism's long-standing presence in print media doesn't justify blindly continuing in it at the same investment level, and that the numbers indicate it is the right move to enter this market, in this way, at this time. Freddy still doesn't fully understand Vivian's resolute short-term focus or her apparent aversion to an expanded perspective, but he tries not to react to his feelings of frustration, knowing that the conversation is far from over.*

*Freddy now receives an e-mail from Trish asking him to come to her office for a meeting the following afternoon. The e-mail does not indicate what she wants to discuss; the subject line says only, 'Let's chat'. The next day at 2:00 pm, Freddy goes to Trish's office. Here's how the conversation goes.*

TRISH:       Good afternoon, Freddy.

FREDDY:    Afternoon.

TRISH:       Your star continues to rise. The senior leadership team has agreed that, since you were instrumental in making the acquisition happen, you should play a key role in managing the transition.

FREDDY:    I'm flattered.

TRISH:       And interested?

FREDDY:    Yes.

TRISH:       Am I right to assume you haven't played such a role in the past?

FREDDY:    No, I never have. What's expected of me?

TRISH:       Well, we've acquired an organization that currently employs 1500 people, in a geography we've ignored until now, in a space in which we have limited expertise. So I'd say there's a lot you can help with.

FREDDY:    Could you be more specific?

TRISH:       The decision to do the acquisition is the first big step. The second big step is to look for synergies across the two companies and make the most of them.

FREDDY:    Are you talking about just IT, or more broadly?

TRISH:       More broadly.

FREDDY:    This is kind of a strange position to be in. All I wanted to do was offer an analysis that would help contribute to the potential decision …

TRISH:       Which you did – very well. So now you've created expectations around yourself. Look, forget what your business card says for now. Unless you don't want this. Are you saying you don't want it?

FREDDY: No. I am definitely interested in playing a bigger role.

TRISH: Okay. My advice to you is to stick with what you did before. It's going to get more complicated, so …

FREDDY: What do you mean by 'more complicated?'

TRISH: Well, this is a bigger deal. The decision being made before was more insular. More self-contained. The integration effort is going to bring you into contact with a lot of folks from a lot of functions, and with a lot of differing perspectives and agendas. There will be a number of different elements and moving parts. You'll have to deal with people offering a lot of different opinions to try to influence you.

FREDDY: And what do I do about that?

TRISH: If you're smart, you listen carefully to any data or logic they provide, but be careful to understand their motives as well. Like I said, your first contribution was well received. Stay on that same track. Present what you know, and if people try to sway you in this direction or that, stay detached.

FREDDY: When you say detached …

TRISH: I mean completely impartial. And you must communicate to them that you're impartial. You said it yourself the other day: What do you ultimately care about?

FREDDY: That I still have a job in a year.

TRISH: Fair enough. Of course, that's the way you can put it only when you're talking to me. The question is: what are you going to say to everyone else? What are you going to tell them about what you believe matters?

FREDDY: I would tell them that what matters is that the company survives long-term.

TRISH: Right. Well, again, I'd say short-term and long-term, because you can't have one without the other.

FREDDY: Sure – certain short-term goals can be used as motivators to establish the right kind of long-term value …

TRISH: I mean, look, I admit I come at this from a slightly narrower view, given that I'm older than you. You're saying you still want to have a job in a year. I'm saying I want to be able to retire within five years. We're saying the same thing but looking at slightly different horizons. The point is we both have the company's best interests at heart. That's why I'm telling you to just keep doing what you did to merit this in the first place, and try to keep the noise around you to a minimum.

FREDDY:   Will do. Thanks.

TRISH:      Anytime. Good luck. You have my support.

## Questions We Asked

1. Have you ever been asked to help integrate two organizations? What was your role, and how did you handle it?
2. What do you think Freddy's main objective should be in the task he's been given? Why?
3. Have you ever been placed in a position of leadership that felt sudden, unexpected or incongruous with your role? What did you do?

## Comments We Got

As a group, our participants were happy about Freddy's continuing opportunity, yet quick to suggest certain behaviours he should adopt in order to make this new level of assignment a success. One thing people seemed to all agree on was that stepping outside of one's comfort zone and assumed duties is virtually *always* a good thing. When given a chance to stretch, they said – quite emphatically in most cases – one should do it, with very few exceptions. It was the strong collective opinion that people are constantly seeking ways to stand out and rise above, therefore such opportunities should hardly be passed up.

At the same time, our participants recognized the challenge facing Freddy: turning analysis on paper into action. The senior management group has made it clear that they are impressed by Freddy's talent at analysing numbers and presenting clear recommendations. Now they are asking him to take on a very different role – leading people. And not just people within the organization he knows well, but people from a company completely unfamiliar to him. Our participants' advice to Freddy was to plunge in with both feet, take up the mantle proudly, make his commitment to the project clear and consistent and establish clear expectations in order to increase the probably of delivering successfully. People were cautiously optimistic about Freddy's ability to satisfy this new request. He has demonstrated clearly that he believes data and objective logic should be used to make value-based decisions. Now such a decision has been made, and it is up to him to translate that decision into human behaviours.

Six themes materialized from the overall responses we received. Here they are, with representative comments included.

## 1. Dive in.

'The quicker and more fully Freddy steps into this new role, the greater acceptance he will get from the team, and the more confidence he will build. By "quick", I do not mean "rush". But by the same token, "floating" could leave room for resistance to build up on all sides. Freddy should try to move at a steady pace but demonstrate a clear commitment to the new assignment.'

'First, Freddy should get a few of the business people in both companies brainstorming on where potential synergies might exist. Given that he helped put the case together for the acquisition, some of this should exist already. Next, he should find a couple of people, again from both sides, to look into the data to see if there is some that suggest synergy value. Finally, he should start thinking about who should be on the integration team to design a leadership structure. It may also be worth considering whether the company should be left as a bolt-on with little synergy action taken, especially during the first few years of the integration. It's during this time that people from the company should spend time learning about, and seeing what could be leveraged into, the existing company while leaving the acquired company to continue to perform as it has before.'

'Freddy should definitely see his being asked to do things outside of his current role as a great opportunity to grow and contribute. I've had a number of "special projects" like this in the past, and while almost all have been painful, they've ultimately been the best career movers. In fact, one of my biggest negative hot buttons is when I ask someone to do something and they respond by saying, "That's not my job". Why would I consider them for special assignments or bigger career opportunities if they aren't interested in doing anything except the job they have?'

## 2. Be willing to lead.

'I was asked to lead a team to put together slides for our board of directors that summarized our business in two slides (!). Slightly ridiculous, and as a marketing manager at the time, I had only some understanding of the data that we would need in order to tell the story. I asked several people who have had experience doing things like this, and we started by making a "data room" with about 40 presentations collected over the years and started thinking about how to tell the story. After a couple of weeks, we had distilled down, but it still lacked clarity. Unfortunately, I realized that in some cases, the only way to move forward is to just push through and make decisions, which I did over one weekend. By Monday morning, we arrived at something that ended up working so well, it was used as a standard template for other businesses to emulate.'

## 3. Be persistent.

'I was a CFO of a wholly-owned subsidiary of my parent company. We acquired a competitor in the same region but in a different country, and the two companies needed to be integrated into one unified operation while remaining separate legal entities. The companies had different histories and contrasting management styles. We needed to find common goals and standardized processes, but this proved very difficult, because the discussion always tended to tilt toward which company's management was "right" or which one was "better". In the end, we found a way to bring the two sides together, but it was a big, difficult challenge.'

'In my current role, I manage a group that consists of three different companies, merged five years ago. Even five years in, I must admit that the three groups really are not particularly well integrated. All three have remarkably different cultures. Since my job is really more about getting the team to function as one team and one culture, it still feels a bit like an integration. I've spent the last several months communicating quite a bit about our role, the need to improve business (in particular operations), and why we can be more successful together. I've also made a big deal about learning the business, and have spent considerable time talking with people who've told me that "it's not usual for guys like you to talk to me". But I've said that I need to understand everything in the business to make the best decisions about it. So for integrating the companies, I've spent time trying to paint a vision of the future and getting ALL of the employees, regardless of their backgrounds, heading in one direction. When there are conflicts, I take the time to hear them out, and then make decisions based on data.'

## 4. Be visible.

'I have been in Freddy's situation once before, and am currently in it a second time. I was certainly better prepared this time around. The hardest part on the first day of such an assignment is to read and go through what you have put forward prior to the acquisition in favour of it. To translate the vision into action plans and carry out the implementation while rallying the team support can be a monstrous task. Freddy seems almost overwhelmed from the get-go. Organizations from the outside look totally different from the inside. There is no time for adapting in such assignments, yet results need to show quickly. I believe the radical approach works best. Change is more tolerated in the first few weeks, since it is expected. The longer the agony lasts of a team waiting to hear what changes you're planning to implement, the more they grow potentially resistant to the change. Freddy should focus on showing quick gains, which will generate trust and alignment between the teams. Sharing the first success with the team is an absolute must.'

'The organization I work for has acquired the IT business of a worldwide manufacturing company, involving 42,000 staff in 40-plus countries. I was requested to lead the IT integration right after the M&A closing. Main drivers were cost optimization and enabling – through one unique IT infrastructure – further business integrations between the incoming teams and existing ones on our side. IT integration on such a scale impacts everyone; being cut off from the IT of your previous organization (mail, unified communication, knowledge management, HR and finance systems, etc.) is often the first/early big shock post-M&A. Speed and quality of execution were key, as was communication about changes and benefits.'

'I think Freddy needs to detach himself from the position of a proponent for the transaction and adopt the role of an impartial leader who is not afraid of admitting gaps he might have had in his supporting elements for the transaction. Transitioning from theory to practice requires constant re-alignment and communication with the hierarchy and the project team. There should be maximum visibility about where the ship is heading, what wrong assumptions may have been made, which ones are verified, and what adjustments are required to deliver the value the transaction is expected to yield.'

## 5. Know what's expected. That makes it easier to deliver.

'Freddy should demand a project charter with clear governance on who the sponsor is, what the reporting lines are and what support he will get, including objectives of the company and what is expected of him in this role. He should discuss with key stakeholders the risks involved and how they can be mitigated. He should seek to drive agreement with the sponsor on budgets and where support will come from within the organization.'

'I would suggest that Freddy build a sort of task force around himself in order to identify the synergies – the real ones, not the theoretical ones! And for each synergy, set a realistic execution timeline and realistic financial estimates. He should also request that top management clarify unambiguously the key strategic objectives of this M&A, so that the synergies he will define with the task force are not in conflict with the means to reach the strategic goal.'

## 6. Learn from others.

'A few years ago, I was moved from Ops to HR. Such moves were common practice at the company I was working for, to expose staff to different situations so they could gain diverse operational and functional experience. Initially, I had a tough time distancing myself from my operational habits. To gain a better understanding of the new role and its context, I spent a couple of weeks working very closely with a highly experienced HR person. From her, I learned the dynamics, practices, key players, etc. in that area. After this initial period of coaching, I started to fully deploy my role, leveraging my Ops experiences but being able to apply it in a situation where I had gained some comfort, familiarity and confidence.'

## Our Thoughts

Only days ago, Freddy was merely trying to adjust to his new GM role and getting to know the players, including his new boss, Vivian, and her boss, Trish. As a result of asking a handful of questions about value and innovation in an early meeting with Vivian and

Trish, he now finds himself thrust into completely new territory: playing a key role in leading the merger of two companies.

This conversation with Trish represents the only time Freddy has seemed apprehensive about the new opportunity. When first asserting that Prism needed to focus more on innovation and value, he was direct and unequivocal. When Trish offered him the opportunity to prepare and present an analysis of the potential Midwest acquisition, he was only too happy to do it. It is easy to see that Freddy's comfort zone involves dealing with spreadsheets and screens. This is not surprising; he comes from a solid engineering training and background, highly accustomed to solving problems that are more analytical in nature.

Things are changing now for Freddy, and he must try to stay the course even as the tasks being handed him take him further and further out of his previous 'safe' space. First, Trish invited him to offer recommendations based on the future-looking value orientation he so strongly defended. Then she shared those recommendations with upper management, quickly boosting Freddy's visibility and status. Now, he is being rewarded by their asking him to become directly engaged in the merger, to help integrate and find synergies across the two companies.

It is indeed a significant opportunity for Freddy. In relation to his existing reputation and relationships, it will not only further establish his credibility and worth within the expanded company, but also (a) actively help him create long-term value for Prism and (b) show his team just how serious he is about the message he is trying to broadcast. This merger represents an ideal opportunity for him to demonstrate to others exactly what he has been talking about to Vivian and Trish.

It will also present a highly valuable learning opportunity. Freddy should indeed plunge in with both feet, knowing that he will likely experience discomfort along the way, but that out of such discomfort often comes substantial growth, an enhanced perspective, new insights and ideas and expanded awareness that could prove invaluable in helping Prism navigate the tough digital transition it is facing. These types of role enlargements are not unusual for those making the transition to general management, especially those who have been able to let go of their own image of themselves as having all the answers. As one gets experience in asking the right questions and approaching problems as an intelligent outsider, taking on new or expanded roles becomes more natural. Freddy is no exception.

Finally, this opportunity can dramatically increase the size of Freddy's network within the new company. He will have an opportunity to interact with, learn from and establish a reputation with a large number of current and newly-acquired colleagues. The ongoing benefits of an expanded network can enhance Freddy's ability to learn, manoeuver and help lead Prism successfully into the future.

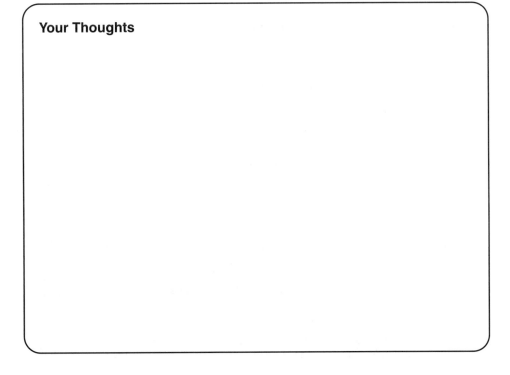

**Your Thoughts**

## NANCY

### The Scenario

*The previous afternoon, Nancy experienced a tense, negative interaction with Dana in the office kitchenette. Dana, claiming she'd been told by Calvin that Nancy was starting to see things her way, offered to enlighten her further on the value perspective any time she might be interested. Nancy felt both betrayed by Calvin – if it was true that he told Dana that Nancy was swinging over to her way of looking at things – and newly resentful of Dana for again behaving in a way she found condescending and arrogant. Nancy feels that she is willing to have a two-way dialogue involving different perspectives, and she knows she has the best interests of The Tipton Group at heart, but she feels that Dana is interested only in proving she is right.*

*Now, Nancy is sitting in front of her computer, looking contemplative and a bit tense. After a few moments, she opens a blank e-mail window. A few moments after that, she types Calvin's name into the 'To' line. After another pause, she then types the one-word subject line, 'Dana'. Finally, after thinking a bit longer, she begins to type in the body of the e-mail.*

*Here's what she ends up writing to Calvin:*

> Calvin,
>
> I ran into Dana yesterday in the lunchroom and she said something that struck me as a bit odd. I was hoping you could help me understand the nature of the conversation and perhaps shed light on it.
>
> Dana offered to help 'teach' me more about what she'd been saying in your office when we had the initial discussion about overall strategic direction and, more specifically, best practices in terms of the use of KPIs, targets, etc. She mentioned that you told her I was 'starting to come over to her side' regarding the way we look at value and define it. Her words were that I was starting to see the concept the way she was trying to explain it to me.
>
> If you'll allow me to speak candidly about this, I felt she was talking down to me, like a child. She seemed to be saying that she really 'gets it', and that I really don't, but

she would be happy to help me try to achieve her level of comprehension and insight. I was confused by this assertion. I tried to suggest that perhaps both sides of the conversation have merit, but she seemed quite closed to this view, instead wanting to make the point clear that I should seek her help in seeing things through the correct lens.

Calvin, I feel it would help me to pursue the dialogue with her if you can help me understand how she seems to have come to this impression. When the three of us spoke in your office, and in the subsequent conversations you and I have had about it, I felt we were having a mutually open discussion and debate about what is clearly an important topic. But that seems to have shifted somehow, and I am seeking clarity on why this has occurred and perhaps what direction you feel would be best for me to take at this point.

Thank you,

Nancy


*After composing the e-mail, Nancy sits back in her chair. Then she leans forward again, reads what she has written, holds her finger over the mouse for a few beats and, after considering for a few moments, clicks Send. Once she sees that the e-mail has gone through, she gets back to the work she was doing.*


## Questions We Asked

1. What do you think of the e-mail Nancy sent Calvin? Would you have written something different? Why or why not?
2. Should Nancy have e-mailed Calvin, talked to him face-to-face, or done something else?
3. What do you see as Nancy's main purpose in sending the e-mail? Is it misguided?


## Comments We Got

Nancy's e-mail to Calvin elicited by far the strongest collective response from our participant community – and not exactly a positive one. Reactions ranged from surprise to disappointment to outright astonishment that Nancy would choose to behave in such a miscalculated way. Most people were stunned that she would not only write this e-mail in the first place, but then allow herself to send it to her immediate supervisor, who surely has better things to do than read a huffy note from a disgruntled staff member. Those who had previously expressed optimism about Nancy's potential as a general manager quickly changed their thinking; those who were already concerned about her abilities simply became firmer in the belief that she may not have what it takes.

Participants made numerous statements – vigorous ones – about the specific elements of Nancy's ill-advised move. First, they reproached her for allowing herself to act based on emotions, something everyone agreed one should never do in the workplace, particularly in a managerial role, and especially a new one in which one is trying to prove herself. Second, they were bowled over by the manner in which she chose to deliver such a message. Though the community roundly agreed she shouldn't send a message like this at all, it agreed even more strongly that she should definitely avoid doing so in an e-mail. Finally, and perhaps most ardently, they felt that moves like this are examples of Nancy digging herself a hole from which she may not be able to climb out unless she immediately changes her approach.

Many participants were of the opinion that Nancy's main objective is to be more elevated than Dana in Calvin's eyes or, more simply, that she has a child's desire to be seen as the preferred one over the other kid playing in the sandbox; and that if she has any chance at all to succeed as a manager, she had better shift her thinking and accompanying behaviour, and fast.

Among the extensive responses to Nancy's e-mail, three broad themes surfaced. Here they are, with a selection of individual comments included (though there were a lot more!).

## 1. Err on the side of diplomacy ...

'Nancy made a big mistake by sending that e-mail to Calvin. If I'd received it, I would have wondered why I'd hired a child! This is a disagreement about views on a topic that is important, but not terribly urgent at the moment. Complaining this way via an e-mail just tells me she isn't mature enough to handle disagreements with co-workers.'

'It would seem that Nancy is venting too much of her frustration to Calvin and is openly expressing criticism about Dana. She is trying to use Calvin to resolve her own conflict/disagreement with Dana. I am unsure what I would have done, as it is never easy to confront openly with someone we feel we have a disagreement ... I might have had initially a discussion with Calvin about my concerns (but not expressed as disagreement) about my impression that Dana is trying to impose her views on me and sought his own views.'

## 2. ... keep emotions out of it ...

'Nancy should have talked to Calvin face-to-face and not sent such a sensitive-sounding e-mail. She sounds like a hurt child.'

'E-mail is not a good tool to convey your emotion. Nancy's e-mail, though she may not have been aware of the fact, was full of anger and complaint. It won't get her anywhere. A manager is expected to manage people who have different opinions. I would not recommend an e-mail in this situation, but if I had to write something, I would include a more specific proposal, like suggesting a new process for making the business plan, crafting the value proposition or dealing with KPIs.'

'Nancy has made a big mistake. Her feelings are hurt, not to mention that she chose entirely the wrong method for making her point. E-mail is really the wrong choice here. Escalations based on emotions are not constructive. I would not have involved Calvin but rather talked to Dana, asking her out for a coffee/

lunch and then continuing the dialogue – even if it's one I didn't particularly like.'

'Nancy's being offended is the obvious reason why she sent this e-mail. She doesn't even seem like she knows what she is trying to achieve by sending it. She seems vulnerable, emotional and erratic in her description of the situation. She has also insinuated several times in her e-mail that Calvin has let her down by siding with Dana, based on what Dana told her. If she was seeking Calvin's support, I think she just lost it.'

'Nancy blew it! All her e-mail reflects is insecurity, and it is full of unnecessary insinuations. It is all about her feelings and has nothing to do with what really matters: the KPI issue, goals and short-term targets versus long-term value. She has just given Dana another reason to prove her point. Nancy has also missed an opportunity to get onside with Dana, as anything she now does will be hampered by the perception that Calvin will have after reading her e-mail. I would have written to Calvin that Dana and I are moving forward in discussing each other's different views and that I've had the chance to hear Dana's side and will be taking the earliest opportunity to meet her so we can drive toward a common solution to share with him. This would have neutralized any assumption that the discussion was over and would give Calvin the sense that Nancy is handling this conflict professionally and keeping the best interests of the company at the forefront. She's done the opposite!'

## 3. ... and don't worry about 'winning'.

'Nancy should never have sent this e-mail after her interaction with Dana. She should have engaged Dana first in a different environment, where she could have been more prepared and where she could manage the discussion on equal footing rather than in a position of disadvantage. After that, and assuming she came out with certain positive outcomes from the discussion, she should share those conclusions with Calvin and seek his support for spelling out a unified vision that incorporates both her and Dana's views.'

'Sending Calvin this e-mail is a major gaffe. If Nancy really wants to discuss the issue with him, she should do it face-to-face. However, she should structure her question so that Calvin can answer yes or no, like, "This is my proposed plan, will you authorize it?" Nancy should not say to her boss, "Dana insulted me – what should I do?" The implication is that she is asking him to get rid of Dana, and she has now created a competition between the two that didn't have to exist.'

'For Nancy to spend time on an e-mail like this – rather than doing meaningful work! – is just a waste. In this kind of situation, I've often acquiesced in the moment and then looked for opportunities to raise the discussion later on, especially after more data has come available and the point can be viewed in new ways. This can lead to different and more meaningful discussion, since it can leave the realm of the theoretical and provide more concrete bearing on the problem at hand. I think Nancy has made a very poor decision.'

'It seems like Nancy sent this e-mail mainly to vent her frustration. Bad idea, and seriously misguided, as she has now put Calvin in a difficult position of "in between" her and Dana.'

'I would think the best course of action is to spend more time with Dana and further the discussion. Bringing something like this up to her supervisor is borderline childish.'

'It looks like Nancy's primary concern is what Calvin thinks of her, and whether or not Dana's discussion about her coming over to her side of the view is making Nancy look like she's dumb for changing her mind. Nancy should worry less about whose opinion gets more attention and more about what the right approach is for the company.'

'Instead of sending petulant e-mails, Nancy should spend more time with Dana and hear her out, certainly before involving

Calvin. If Dana really does have a valid viewpoint, it's best for Nancy to fully understand it before escalating.'

## Our Thoughts

Nothing can more clearly demonstrate the importance of emotional intelligence than the e-mail sent from Nancy to Calvin. Because of her lack of self-awareness and her inability to reflect on how Dana made her feel and why, Nancy has made a serious blunder. First, as so many of our contributors pointed out, though the e-mail is eloquently written, its basic message is, to say the least, underwhelming: *One of my colleagues made me feel bad, and I'd like you to do something about it.* Calvin is an experienced manager; he will easily recognize this e-mail for what it is. Nancy's attempt to couch it in a desire to 'better understand' what Dana was trying to say to her will come across as a veiled desire to either (a) get Dana in trouble with the boss or (b) paint Dana in a negative light in Calvin's eyes.

Neither result is one that will help Nancy improve in her role. Nancy's performance as a manager should be about *Nancy*, not Dana. In sending this message to her boss, Nancy is demonstrating all the wrong things: that she reacts emotionally; that she is impulsive; that she is more focused on others than on herself; and, by far the worst of all, that she has the wrong priorities. Calvin has already had one discussion with Nancy in which he tried to tell her, in a fairly direct manner, that the only thing that matters to him is having a team whose members share the goal of creating sustainable value for The Tipton Group. Nancy's note communicates virtually the opposite message. It has only to do with her individual feelings and personality dynamics, and it has nothing to do with the organization or how to create value on its behalf.

Furthermore, Calvin is not going to take kindly to the idea that Nancy is going to come to him with trivial issues like this in the future. Someone at Nancy's level should have by now learned not only how to deal with personality differences, but also how to use them to the company's benefit, by maximizing complementary skills and mutual learning.

In her previous job at Whitesands, Nancy operated in somewhat of a vacuum. Heading a team that was largely siloed, she had little need to interact with other peers or superiors. She has had limited experience dealing with the manifold personal dynamics that exist at a larger, more interconnected firm like The Tipton Group, and this inexperience is showing.

Nancy needs to find someone with whom she can discuss such issues. If she had had a coach, someone to talk to who could ask the right questions and focus Nancy on her own insecurities and anxieties, she would most likely never have written such an e-mail. This is why transitions need to be supported by development and coaching. Nancy was temporarily lost and had no one to turn to, so she turned to her boss, but in an inappropriate way. With this e-mail, she is not approaching Calvin as coach or mentor, but as the referee in a childish game of 'Who do you like better?'

So what can Nancy do now that she has sent the ill-conceived e-mail? She should approach Calvin immediately and apologize for temporarily letting her emotions get the better of her. If she is lucky, Calvin is the type of boss who will use this as an opportunity to coach Nancy and explore what kind of support she could benefit from in her development. At a minimum, Nancy ought to seek out someone to talk to who has been through the transition themselves (excluding Dana). Nancy cannot continue to view Dana as the thorn in her side, or anyone else as a potential nemesis threatening to bring her down. Such an attitude will surely make it impossible for Nancy to succeed at just about any level of the company, and certainly not at a GM level, where she needs to develop expertise at managing relationships up, down and across.

Nancy can benefit from taking herself back a few conversations, particularly to when she and Calvin were starting to discuss the nature of value creation and the importance of objectivity. She must practice impartiality not only with data, but also with people. At the moment, she is disposed to take things personally and spend an unwarranted amount of time thinking about how other people see and treat her. It is vital that she instead start thinking about everyone around her – including Dana, Calvin, her direct reports, senior leadership and everyone else – as members of the same team in pursuit of a common goal.

**Your Thoughts**

# HUGO

## The Scenario

*Days earlier, Hugo was called into a meeting with Dino and Peter Falken-*
*berg, Hugo's VP counterpart for Asia. Peter, with his hardware background,*
*was, to say the least, rough around the edges, leaving Hugo virtually*
*speechless. Dino told Hugo and Peter that he wanted them to plan a confer-*
*ence for their combined teams sometime over the next two months. Hugo*
*left the meeting a bit baffled by Peter's manner.*

*Hugo e-mails Dino requesting time for a brief chat. Dino responds imme-*
*diately, telling Hugo he is just finishing a conference call but is available*
*in 20 minutes. Promptly 20 minutes later, Hugo approaches Dino's office.*
*Dino's executive assistant tells Hugo that he is off the call and available.*
*Hugo enters. Here's how their exchange proceeds.*

DINO:    Good morning, Hugo. What's up?

HUGO:    Dino, I wanted to ask your advice about something. I've been discussing with my team our strategic planning goals for the next 24
months, and there is some dissension. People have strong opinions. Contrasting ones.

DINO:    Let me ask you a question. What's your goal in these discussions?

HUGO:    To drive agreement among the group?

DINO:    Are you asking me or telling me?

HUGO:    I suppose I want to get everyone on the same page.

DINO:    Can you define that better?

HUGO:    I want us to agree on the right approach.

DINO:    And do you feel you're communicating that goal successfully?

HUGO:    Yes and no. I'm not sure I'd describe the discussion as healthy.
There are a lot of opinions being thrown around, with not much
resolution or agreement.

DINO:    I would humbly suggest that the first thing you need to convince
them of – and yourself – is that that word you just said, *opinions*,
is a hazardous word.

HUGO:    How do you mean?

DINO:    Remember our discussion about the Discounted Expected Free Cash Flows?

HUGO:    Yes.

DINO:    Do you buy into it?

HUGO:    Certainly.

DINO:    What's the benefit of it?

HUGO:    Well, it's objective.

DINO:    Instead of?

HUGO:    Subjective.

DINO:    And opinions are?

HUGO:    Subjective.

DINO:    So what purpose do they serve?

HUGO:    None, I guess.

DINO:    So one of your main tasks is to convince those in your charge that you aren't interested in their opinions. You're interested in their interpretation of data. Their read of the information and what it tells us.

HUGO:    Isn't that the same as opinions?

DINO:    What do you think of my shirt?

HUGO:    What?

DINO:    What do you think of my shirt?

HUGO:    Um, it's very nice.

DINO:    That's an opinion. But if I asked you whether a person should shop at the store where I bought the shirt, would you say yes or no?

HUGO:    Neither.

DINO:    Why not?

HUGO:    I'd want to know more about the store first.

DINO:    Yes. You'd want data, and then you could offer an interpretation of it. You need to convince your team of that distinction. You can invite people's reading of the data. But opinions have no place.

HUGO:    I'm not sure I'm clear on the difference.

DINO:    Opinions have a personal element. They advance an agenda, or serve a hidden goal, or reflect a bias. Interpretations of data are based in fact. The first translates to, 'This is what I believe.' The second translates to, 'This is what I feel the information is saying.' And it needs to come from you first. Your own statements have to be bias-free, non-leading, non-positioning.

HUGO: How do I encourage the varying perspectives while discouraging opinions?

DINO: Make it clear that the goal isn't for anyone to emerge as victor, or for anyone's solution to be accepted as the right one. As a group, you're seeking to reach a value-based decision, which is the only way to achieve sustainable health and success. Multiple perspectives are good. People thinking that their view should be the one that 'wins' is bad, and ultimately has no place here. Look at it this way. If everyone is always trying to get their opinion to be the accepted one, what is the result for AMR as a company? Do we create value in this way?

HUGO: No. The result would be …

DINO: At some point, catastrophic. No company can survive that way, because it means opinion-based decisions are being made all the time, at the expense of a view toward real, long-term value. It isn't possible to operate that way and continue to survive. Do you understand what I'm saying?

HUGO: I think I do. Perspectives, yes. Opinions, no …

DINO: You took the words right out of my mouth.

## Questions We Asked

1. Have you ever been in a leadership position where you found it difficult to keep people's opinions or personal agendas separate from the need to solve a problem? What approach did you take? Was it successful?

2. Have you ever worked for someone who was very good at, or very poor at, minimizing biases and upholding the importance of objectivity? What did this person do to make them good or bad at it?

3. Have you ever been around a leader who was able to show people respect while at the same rejecting their right to have 'opinions'? How did they do this?

## Comments We Got

A large number of our participants reported having been in situations involving colleagues or, more often, superiors, who, whether overtly or not, made decisions based on opinions, biases or personal agendas. In some cases, people said that little could be done in response, given the person's position or influence. In other cases, positive examples were given of significant changes occurring because these opinions, biases and agendas were, either in the form of personnel change or a shift in processes, eliminated. Many stressed the importance of sticking to facts, using data neutrally, and using information as a means of advancing the only proper agenda – the value agenda – everywhere in the organization.

Reassuringly, an equal number of participants spoke of immediate supervisors, colleagues they have observed in action, or senior mentors elsewhere in the organization who have provided strong examples of minimizing opinions while driving collective productivity toward common, value-based goals. In describing different types of effective leaders, numerous members of our participant community described something very important that all of these people had in common: each of them had a way of making people feel involved in achieving the shared objective, but at the same time they managed to send a clear message that any personal stake, including their own, was immaterial. These kinds of leaders, our participants said, were encouraging and challenging in the proper balance, because they recognized the importance of participation and engagement from their teams, but they sent a clear message that 'opinions' would be considered only when they weren't really opinions at all.

The general responses we received centred around three themes. Here they are, along with some of the most relevant comments.

### 1. The first agenda to get rid of is your own.

'I believe one of the best things a manager can do is focus on the content or process – that is, the what or the how – instead of on positions – the who. I also think it's important to be honest with yourself and to ask, before you worry about other people's agendas, whether you yourself have one that you need to put aside.'

'I have found often that when people are under high pressure or in complex situations, and/or feeling structural decisions may be out of their reach, they resort to giving opinions and pushing personal agendas. True leaders stay responsible and accountable to the programme or initiative even under pressure or uncertainty.'

'Early in my career, I would frequently have discussions based on opinions or statements, and I would try to get as many supporters as possible to help me "win" the argument. This is why I can now recognize it when it happens! These days, I address things in concrete terms: where are the facts, why do you say this, is this your opinion, what is it based on, how are you affected personally, and does that play a role in reaching your opinion?'

'I recently worked for someone who was put in a COO-type role, but who was clearly in over his head. He unfortunately responded to this pressure by spending lots of time trying to build the picture of a reality that represented him in a positive light. He portrayed it to management at a global executive level on more than one occasion to try to win their favour. To make matters worse, he could not stand people's input unless they happened to align with this fabricated reality. He did not tolerate confrontation or anyone challenging his analyses, and eventually he started denying the stories clearly told by hard data. Needless to say, he was ultimately removed from the role.'

**2. Get rid of anyone else's, too.**

'I have had the fortune of being able to work with people who were not only highly data-oriented but who can also usually smell when people are trying to "shape" data or tell a persuasive story rather than report results. Often their skill is in asking the kinds of questions that force someone to reconsider their position. It's great when you can see people melting under the heat!'

'I worked with a board chairman who was very good at minimizing biases. He accomplished this by never showing a personal interest in the outcome of discussions, only an interest in the most effective common solution.'

'My group CIO does a good job of this. He allows people to express their opinions to help put them at ease and make them feel involved, but he always reminds them that their opinions are only worthwhile and trustworthy if backed up by hard analysis. He often plays Devil's Advocate, too, to push us to think, model, process and act upon a basis of tangible reasoning.'

'I am always surprised and enthusiastic to meet executives who are less interested in their own careers than in the common interest of the company or its stakeholders.'

'As a leader in technical service, I frequently ran into people, more senior than me, as well as with PhDs in the sciences, whose approach to design was to run tons of experiments and then look at the data the way one might look for a needle in a haystack. Most of the time, these approaches to problem-solving were based on opinions or, worse, on experiments that were designed to underscore personal agendas. Finally the leader in our R&D group was changed, and he thankfully introduced a data-based approach to research. A lot of good work was done, and some personal pet projects were killed after it was shown that the data had no potential for value.'

'My marketing manager is very good at re-directing discussions back toward facts, data and processes. It has to be said, though, that he has been accused of not displaying the right level of empathy.'

**3. Rally people around goals.**

'Aligning people around a set of common, tangible short-term objectives that result from fact-based analyses can often help build momentum around tangible/real results, thus motivating people to focus on a meaningful longer-term goal.'

'It's a long process to move from "opinion without data" to "opinion supported by data". I try to focus on the data, making everyone feel involved and important.'

'Every team member wants to feel a part of the project success. One way to do this is to try to frame discussions and debates within a broad or general perspective, instead of any one person's unique or personal experience playing a role.'

## Our Thoughts

The first critical step in Hugo's evolution as a GM was to begin to appreciate the purpose of seeking value in the proper way, from the right perspective, and using the proper tools. He has also, largely as a result of Dino's guidance, achieved important insights into the different hats he must now wear, the flexible ways in which he must now communicate with different groups, and the varying sensitivities he must now be aware of in order to execute his job successfully.

With Hugo having gained some confidence and starting to climb a demanding learning curve, he comes up against a new challenge: how to involve those on his team in important discussions and decisions without inviting their opinions. He approaches Dino, who has given his sound advice to this point, asking how to manage situations in which people offer views and opinions, often in contrast to one another, each of them seeking 'air time'. As a functional leader in his previous role, Hugo did not find himself in the position of having to deal with this very sensitive issue. Everyone, after all, wants to be heard, most people want to have their idea favoured, and human instinct tells us to argue a point until the other person concedes.

While Hugo understands well at this point that the only justifiable arguments are those based in facts and data, he is less skilled at handling the human element that has now come to the forefront of his role. Those on his team are trying to 'win' the argument or have their view be the one held out as the 'best' one or the 'right' one. What Hugo continues to have in his corner is the willingness to learn, the openness to listen, the desire to succeed and the conviction that creating long-term value for the organization will translate into success for himself. As Dino exhorts him to do, Hugo must stay focused on this goal, and he must communicate that focus to everyone else around him, not least those who report to him.

Rather than asking for opinions, he should encourage his people to ask good questions. Good questions lead to important answers and, often, to a new interpretation of data, or a different lens into the same information that has been looked at before. He should advise them to try to stay away from positional or leading statements. He must adopt a fair process approach, in which people are allowed to be heard, but opinions are placed to the side and kept there. Hugo does not seem to be focused on building his own status or painting himself in a favourable light, which speaks well to his potential as a manager. His goal now must be to leverage people's knowledge, experience and insights while encouraging them to leave their biases and opinions at the door.

**Your Thoughts**

\* \* \*

## Overall Discussion

In this chapter, each of our GMs encountered an issue involving the people they work with. Freddy is being thrust into an increasingly prominent role to exploit the synergies with the Midwest company that Prism is acquiring; Nancy is trying to figure out what to do with a peer whom she feels is toxic; and Hugo is discovering the complexity of leading a team of human beings with emotions and opinions. All three are learning, in different ways, that to ultimately create value, they must manage a multiplicity of perspectives combined with an absence of opinion. They are also learning that making effective management decisions means upholding fair process even amid uncertainty, dissension or turmoil. Whether faced with a sensitive situation, a difficult colleague or an array of views, Freddy, Nancy and Hugo must maintain decision-making clarity while maintaining the focus of those around them on a value-based, data-driven path.

In their *Harvard Business Review* article on Fair Process,[1] authors Chan Kim and Renée Mauborgne describe the differences between distributive justice and procedural justice. Distributive justice concerns itself with resource allocation, economic incentives and organizational structure to create compulsory cooperation in a team to meet expectations. Organizations that rely heavily on KPI targets often do so because their management style embraces the standard concerns of distributive justice: budgets (resource allocation), rewards (economic incentives) and authority (organizational structure). In such management systems, tremendous organizational effort is put into ensuring that the indicators meet the targets, regardless of the reliability of these indicators or the relevance of the targets to the long-term health of the company.

[1]W. Chan Kim and Renee Mauborgne, 'Fair Process: Managing in the Knowledge Economy,' *Harvard Business Review*, January 2003: pp. 127–136.

Procedural justice, on the other hand, concerns itself with a fair process of engagement, explanation and expectation clarity to create voluntary cooperation to create value. This management style centres less around compulsory cooperation to achieve specific targets and is more concerned with the process by which cooperation happens and decisions are made.

Our GMs might assume that, given a test to their management skills – whether in the form of a stretch assignment, a difficult colleague or a communication challenge – they should demonstrate their ability to dominate or assert, or create compulsory cooperation to meet stated targets. But they will quickly come to see that, in a value-based environment, one leads by making sound decisions, explaining them clearly and staying on message. Sound decisions come from engaging the team to explore options, offering objective criteria by which options will be judged and establishing clarity around the expectations of execution. Keeping opinions away from the centre of discussion frees the team to objectively evaluate whether the execution is bringing about the expected outcomes, rather than spending their time fabricating indicators to justify a certain decision.

## Key Questions to Ask Yourself

1. When you experience resistance from others to playing political games, are you nonetheless able to manoeuver and manage relationships to maintain your own effectiveness and, in the eyes of others, continue to manage via fair process?
2. Do you consciously build and manage your network, within your organization as well as outside of it, in order to ensure you have access to knowledge, resources and relationships which will prove helpful in ensuring you are able to both continue to learn

how to manage for value creation and also have the ability and resources to do so as your environment changes?

3. Do you regularly 'step back' from your role and your relationships with others and try to visualize how others see you, and imagine how they might interpret your words, actions and behaviours towards them and others?

# Section 3
# Managing Yourself

# Chapter 7

# Taking the Reins

## FREDDY

### The Scenario

*The previous week, Trish called Freddy to her office to inform him that Prism's senior management wanted him to play an expanded role in the acquisition of, and merger with, the Midwest company. She encouraged him to accept the invitation to do so, and at the same time cautioned him that, whereas he is currently learning how to deal with the many opinions of those in the immediate environment, in taking on this new responsibility he will in addition have to deal with the opinions – and emotions – of those in the company being acquired.*

*It will be difficult, she tells him. He will find himself in the middle of many sensitive, loaded conversations. But if he sticks to his focus on a long-term value orientation, he will do fine. It will be essential, she tells him, to continue to communicate this orientation and to make very clear his own impartiality. She adds two important notes: first, that Freddy has her support; and second, that she endorses the value perspective.*

*Freddy accepts senior management's invitation to take on the expanded duties. After his first meeting with those from the Midwest side, he goes directly to Trish's office. He knocks on the door. She looks up from her desk. Freddy enters and closes the door behind him. Here's how their conversation goes.*

FREDDY:  Boy, were you right.

TRISH:    About what?

FREDDY:  Opinions.

TRISH:    What about them?

FREDDY:  There are a lot of people with them.

TRISH:    I guess you had your first merger meeting?

FREDDY:  I just got off a videoconference with some of the key Chicago leadership.

TRISH:    Have a seat.

          *(Freddy sits)*

          They're in a tough spot. They feel vulnerable because they're being taken over, but they also feel the need to be vocal and assert themselves so they don't get completely steamrolled.

FREDDY:  That's about right.

TRISH:    How did it go?

FREDDY:  I didn't feel I was overly effective. Felt myself dancing a lot.

TRISH:    Dancing?

FREDDY:  Scrambling. Speaking in vague terms. Backtracking.

TRISH:    Did you feel sorry for them?

FREDDY:  How do you mean?

TRISH:    Did you feel sympathy for their position?

FREDDY:  Sympathy? I didn't really think of it that way. More like anxiety than sympathy. They were kind of timid one minute, then kind of aggressive the next. I would have to say it put me on edge.

TRISH:    It's harder being on their side of the table. Wouldn't you agree?

FREDDY:  Yes, I suppose it is. I wanted to talk about the potential synergies between the two companies, but I think they're more interested in talking about how many roles might be lost. They seem very concerned that we're going to tear apart something they've spent years building up.

TRISH:    So is it fair to say you felt resistance from them?

FREDDY:  Yes.

TRISH:    Even resentment, maybe?

FREDDY:  Uh-huh. That's absolutely accurate.

TRISH:    How do you think you would feel in their shoes?

FREDDY: The exact same way they feel, I guess.

TRISH: Right. So your challenge is to capture the knowledge and experience while trying to minimize the personal stuff. It will take time. This is not an overnight exercise.

FREDDY: Any suggestions in the meantime?

TRISH: Well, I can't tell you how to deal with the emotional issues, which are very real – I think that's a matter for the Communications people – but from a business perspective, my advice is to keep it scientific.

FREDDY: Scientific?

TRISH: Try to understand where they're coming from. Talk to the Comms folks about how you can utilize empathy to forge a stronger rapport. But at the same time, remember that the objective here isn't to save jobs, it's to create meaningful ones.

FREDDY: That isn't an easy message to deliver.

TRISH: It certainly isn't. You can't ignore the fact that they're going to be fearful and, in a lot of cases, angry – but it's not up to you to solve that for them. You need to try to be empathetic without being sympathetic.

FREDDY: You're losing me.

TRISH: Step into their shoes as much as you can. They're people, and they're going to have feelings about this. But in terms of the business – in terms of combining their knowledge and experience with ours – think of it as employing the scientific method. We develop hypotheses about potential results, and then we test them.

FREDDY: You make it sound like a chemistry experiment.

TRISH: I'll get you a lab coat for Christmas.

## Questions We Asked

1. How do you think Freddy should manage his interactions with the key players from the company Prism has acquired?
2. How do you interpret Trish's advice about applying a 'scientific' approach and using hypotheses to drive value?

3. Have you ever been in a position like Freddy's, where it was important to exhibit empathy but also to avoid solving emotional issues or managing people's personal feelings? How did you handle the situation?

## Comments We Got

Freddy must feel in some ways as though he is in the twilight zone. Just a short time ago, he was merely one of Prism's functional IT leaders. Now, he is sitting across the table from the leadership team of a company in Chicago which Prism has just acquired, discussing synergies between the two entities.

No matter how surreal Freddy may be finding his quick and unexpected journey, our participant community's collective message to him was unequivocal: go with it. People felt that Freddy has been handed a rare opportunity, and that for him to reject or squander it would be equivalent to career suicide. While overall comments were sympathetic toward Freddy's plight, the specific advice to him was not. Most participants advised him to be uncompromisingly consistent in his role on Prism's behalf and in his message of value to both sides.

People also had strong views about how he should conduct himself now that he has been moved 'from the frying pan into the fire' – from performing an analysis of the investment opportunity to talking face to face with those who are worried that they may not have a job to go to at the end of the day, or week, or month. It was clearly recognized that this is brand new territory for Freddy. He has embraced his ascent to this point, and he has welcomed the opportunity to stretch beyond his usual comfort zone. But, as many people saw from his unannounced meeting with Trish, he is now treading in different, more sensitive waters, and is feeling decidedly less comfortable now that the human element has been intensified. Freddy is, most agreed, a nice guy, very human, and likely to respond strongly to emotional reactions from others.

Recognizing this, the most common advice to Freddy was to try his best to stick to the business discussion. The fact that he is in the middle of an emotionally-loaded situation was, almost everyone felt, even more reason for him to try to remind himself of the purpose of his role: to maximize synergies between the companies. As long as he can find it within himself to do that, the community seemed to agree, he will continue to earn his management stripes.

Three themes emerged from the overall responses received. Here they are, with illustrative comments.

## 1. Broadcast the value message.

'Freddy should make every effort to get everyone on both sides to recognize the new exciting opportunity, to understand the goals, and to participate in achieving them. Everyone needs to understand that they have only two options: get on board or leave. There is no option for things to remain the way they have been.'

'Freddy has been handed a true leadership opportunity, and he should take advantage of it by promoting and demonstrating the possibility for success in the new environment. There is almost nothing you can do about people's emotions, but you can try to focus them on the improved alternatives ahead that will result from a value orientation. People who do not buy into the message, even after proper efforts to communicate it have been undertaken, should leave.'

'Freddy should interact individually with the key players on both sides and conduct group sessions as well. He should carefully question each of the key players in order to understand their role and influence. He should also give the key players from the acquired company the chance to learn about Prism, its processes, its culture and its ways of conducting business to help reduce their anxiety toward an unknown environment. He should clarify the expected post-M&A synergies and involve the key players in the process of planning to maximize them. This would not only leverage useful knowledge and experience but also enable key players to find new purpose and meaningful roles within the new organization, as Trish suggests. Finally, Freddy should emphasize his interaction with the key players as an ambassador of Prism. Whatever the culture of Prism, he should portray it strictly.'

## 2. Keep ego and emotion to the side.

'It will be of utmost importance for Freddy to avoid showing emotion to the key players on both sides, who are themselves likely very emotional, as are those mostly impacted by the change. He must lead by example by being unemotional – empathic but not sympathetic – thus hopefully encouraging similar behaviour in the key players themselves, who will then feel empowered to focus on the opportunity ahead.'

'Several of the town halls I hosted upon coming into my new job found me having to answer questions from some very anxious/angry people. Why is there ANOTHER global business director? Why not from a different department? Why are you thinking about changing so much? Why are we not getting money out of this in the short term? I reminded myself again and again to remain objective, try to think about the questions from their perspectives, and answer in the context of today's reality and the positive opportunities resulting from it.'

## 3. Stick to the facts.

'Freddy earned his current responsibility by focusing on the data, and he should continue to do so, making the financial case for value creation between the two companies. He should try to involve key people from the acquired company and orient them to a 'hypothesis-test-conclude' approach. Above all, he needs to stay focused on the task, and not on the unknowns or fears.'

'My thinking is that Freddy should acknowledge a common interest in preserving the acquired company's value to the market but propose the bigger benefits to be won – using data.'

## Our Thoughts

Coming out of his first meeting with the leadership of the acquired company, Freddy seems a bit like a wide-eyed child wondering what he may have gotten himself into. Such discussions are difficult even for those who have experience handling them. For Freddy, these kinds of meetings are completely new, making them that much harder, and making him feel that much more inexpert.

Freddy's situation is a perfect illustration of the two different approaches to management we discussed in the previous chapter: distributive justice versus procedural justice. The managers from the acquired company will naturally start off with a distributive justice mindset, demonstrating concerns over resource allocation, economic incentives and organizational structure. Their primary concern will be 'protecting their share'. There will be no way to simultaneously address their distributive justice concerns while ensuring that the appropriate synergies are explored to create the most value from this acquisition. Under a distributive justice mindset, things quickly become political and stay that way.

Freddy needs to try to quickly change their focus towards procedural justice and fair process. He must engage them to explore options, explain the objective (value) criteria that will be used to evaluate options, and then clarify the expectations around execution. There is no going back.

To pull this off, Freddy must be able to maintain his objectivity and empathy with the team across the table. A fair-process approach can work only if Freddy remains focused on the message of value creation. He must go back to his very first conversation with Vivian and Trish, in which the trio debated Prism's long-term strategy, and remind himself how and why he arrived at this position in the first place. It was because he argued fervently for a value orientation and an innovation mindset. He must stick to this message now more than ever.

People will be angry. They will be bitter and resentful about what is happening beyond their control. There will be a profusion of different feelings in the room during every discussion. But Freddy must remember that, at least as far as his role goes, only one message matters: the message that they are all here to work together so that both companies will end up stronger, healthier and more resilient as a result of the merger. Freddy cannot address their distributive justice concerns, and he should avoid at all costs being dragged into such a discussion. Instead, he must focus on fair process and procedural justice and, eventually, if he can convince them that he is objective in this regard, he will be in a good position to eventually bring them around to a similar mindset.

Trish's suggestion to use a hypothesis-based approach is entirely consistent with fair process. Options to be explored are treated as hypotheses and then tested rigorously and objectively. Hypotheses mean detachment; they are automatically unprejudiced, since they don't allow room for opinions or beliefs. The more Freddy can employ this method, the more he will be able to carry out his duties in the context of the merger without letting emotions hijack the process.

What will be especially difficult for Freddy is to be simultaneously empathetic and objective. But by doing so, he will be able to find the words and the tone needed to keep people open and communicating, which is necessary to ensure that the right information will become available to guide the integration successfully and keep people on-side even though they will be anxious, and perhaps even hostile, during the merger. It is Freddy's job to manage the emotions of others in order to keep them focused on the short-term objective of a successful integration to achieve the long-term objective of value creation for the company. This requires first becoming the manager of his own emotions.

Freddy has been handed a tough role to play. But those in positions of power and authority at Prism believe he is the right choice to play it, and his only decision should be to embrace it and make the most of it. He is not in this position because of accidental fortune. He is in this position because he decided to become vocal about the company's future strategy and its need to change mentality if it were to survive. Now he has been given an opportunity to demonstrate that belief in actions, on a visible stage, in a high-pressure environment. Seizing this opportunity can not only make Freddy a better manager and leader, but it can also help him do exactly what he has been asking to do since his first conversation with Trish: create value for the organization.

**Your Thoughts**

# NANCY

## The Scenario

*After her strained interaction with Dana in the office kitchenette the previous afternoon, Nancy sent Calvin an e-mail giving her interpretation of what had happened. In it, she expressed confusion and mild indignation at Dana's suggestion to help teach her more about value and proper use of targets and indicators. She also noted Dana's mentioning that Calvin had said Nancy was coming over to Dana's side. Nancy asked Calvin to help her understand what may have transpired, not very successfully couching her annoyance and feeling of Dana's effrontery.*

*Nancy now sees a new e-mail ding into her Inbox, addressed to her and Dana. The e-mail is from Calvin and has the subject line, 'Chat'. The body of the e-mail reads:*

> Dear Dana and Nancy,
>
> I'd like you to swing by my office at 2:30 pm today for a brief discussion. Please be prompt.
>
> Thanking you and with best wishes,
>
> Calvin

*Nancy sits at her desk for a while, staring at the e-mail. She re-reads it several times, trying to unearth a clue from Calvin's words as to the nature of the discussion he is planning. She sits back in her chair and thinks back over all recent conversations with him, with Dana, and with him about Dana. She tries to remember if she has spoken to any of her other colleagues about her issues with Dana. Then she scrolls through her e-mail folders and reads through any e-mails that she has sent Dana, Dana has sent her, Calvin has sent Dana with her copied, Calvin has sent her with Dana copied, or others have sent involving one or both of them.*

*Nancy exhales in frustration, unable to suss out Calvin's intention. She wonders whether he is going to bring up the e-mail she sent him the day before, about her interaction with Dana and her request for suggestions as to how to optimize the relationship between the two of them, for the benefit of the team and the organization. She isn't completely familiar with Calvin's style yet, so she doesn't know if he's the type of boss who might force people to confront issues head-on and in person. Maybe. Perhaps he is going to ask Dana to answer for the aggressive manner in which she has been treating Nancy and remind her that people need to get along well in a company in order to do good work together.*

*Nancy goes to have lunch to try and clear her head. When she returns, she reads Calvin's e-mail a few more times. Finally she puts it aside, does some work, and waits for 2:30. At 2:25, she goes to Calvin's office, hoping to speak with him for a few minutes before Dana arrives. But Calvin's assistant tells Nancy that he would like her to wait until Dana has arrived as well.*

*Five minutes later, Dana arrives. She greets Nancy, who says hello back. The door to Calvin's office opens, and, with a smile, he says good afternoon and invites the two of them in. Here's how the conversation goes.*

CALVIN: Please sit down, ladies. Let's talk.

DANA: Sure. What about?

CALVIN: Have a seat, Dana. We won't take long. I know you both have important work to do.
*(Dana and Nancy sit in opposite chairs across from Calvin's desk. He crosses his hands, smiles, and looks back and forth between them.)*

CALVIN: Dana. Nancy. Well, the sooner we address this, the better. Listen, I consider you both highly valuable assets to this team. You know that, right?

NANCY: Yes.

DANA: Of course.

CALVIN: And you know that I think you both bring different things to the table that contribute equally to the success of this team. Are you aware of this fact, too?

DANA: Mm-hm.

NANCY: I think so.

CALVIN: Good – I'm glad that's clear. Without either one of you, we'd be a lot worse off. At the same time, I am worried.

DANA: Why?

CALVIN:   Because you're both demonstrating too much concern about what I think of your views, and about what each of you thinks of the other's views as well.

NANCY:   Shouldn't we care what you think of our views?

CALVIN:   No, you shouldn't. You shouldn't even care what you think of your own views. Because they're your *views*. Your *beliefs*. Your *opinions*. What they are not is facts.

DANA:    May I say something?

CALVIN:   Of course.

DANA:    What you're saying is what I was trying to explain to Nancy yesterday, when we were talking about KPIs in contrast to real value.

NANCY:   I really don't think this conversation is about –

CALVIN:   Dana, in the context of this discussion, that's beside the point. I wish to make it much simpler for both of you, so that you can make the most of your working relationship and leverage each other's natural talents and skills.

          *(Nancy and Dana look at each other. Dana maintains a businesslike expression. Nancy forces a smile.)*

CALVIN:   The truth is that there are only three things I want from both of you. The first is to make decisions that you believe are sound, based on data. The second is to be able to clearly explain those decisions – again, based on the data. The third is to ensure that you remove any personal stake from those decisions.

NANCY:   But you don't mean entirely, right? I mean, how is it possible to completely remove yourself from any decision?

CALVIN:   I do mean entirely, Nancy. Not only entirely, but permanently. This is a very, very important point for you to understand. We can only create real change, and be successful in the long term, if everyone has the same approach. One person making decisions based on their own biases or opinions can affect the whole organization. If one person does it, then the next is forced to do it, as a way of competing. A domino effect inevitably takes hold. It won't take long after that before the company is no more.

DANA:    What is it that you're asking from us?

CALVIN:   I want to know that you're both aware that I don't care which of you is right or wrong about a given topic or decision. I care about how and why you make decisions, and I care about the ways in which you back them up. We all need to come at things from a shared perspective. Me, you, everyone else. Like I said, that is the only way it works in the long term.

NANCY: The only way what works?

CALVIN: The quest for value. You can't get there if people let their own egos get in the way. Use your talent, use your skill, use your knowledge – but leave your egos out of it. Okay?

NANCY: Okay …

DANA: Absolutely.

CALVIN: Great. Thanks for listening. That's all.

NANCY: Thank you, Calvin. I appreciate your raising this matter.

DANA: Yes, thanks – great meeting.

*(Nancy and Dana both get up and exit Calvin's office.)*

## Questions We Asked

1. What internal change do you think Nancy needs to make to realize her potential as a GM?
2. In your role, how much do you rely on what you 'think'? Is this encouraged or not?
3. Do you think it's possible to be truly objective in decision making, with a total lack of ego?

## Comments We Got

Our participants' attitude about Nancy in this chapter started to shift from head-shaking bewilderment to collective compassion. People seemed to feel that a major factor in her undercurrent of emotionality was her lack of self-esteem. Several made the point that if Nancy were to focus more on learning the business inside-out and committing to supporting her decisions based on a value orientation, she would necessarily have less time to spend on worrying about what others – like Dana – think, or the manner in which they behave.

The majority of participants agreed that Nancy needs to somehow detach herself from her feelings and concentrate more on her contribution to the health and growth of The Tipton Group through value-based decision-making, but people offered diverse suggestions for how she should go about it. Some encouraged her to focus on the relationship with Calvin and to try to emulate his leadership style and unshakeable focus on value. Others felt it paramount that Nancy does introspective work and finds a way to remove her emotions from her work before she finds herself out of a job, or at least demoted from her GM role. Still others were of the keen opinion that Nancy will only be able to untether herself from her emotions if she focuses fully on the business. Once she feels she is an expert, said this group, she will feel more confident, and once she feels more confident, she will develop the courage to accept different kinds of attitudes and behaviours from others – and once she does that, she will no longer have trouble maintaining a Calvin-type focus on the pursuit of value for the company, because she will no longer hold up as her foremost concern what other people think of her.

Our participants' overall responses to the conversation among Calvin, Nancy and Dana centred around three themes. Here they are, including many of the more notable comments.

## 1. There should be no 'you' in your decisions.

'I feel Nancy needs to distance herself from her decisions and try to be more neutral. She seems to be equating how she does at her job with who she is as a person.'

'Nancy is too concerned with what Calvin thinks about her. While it's important for her to keep him informed, her focus on his perception of her may lead to poor decision-making on her part. She should focus instead on being able to explain her decisions well, and on the basis of data. If Calvin has a vested interest in some of these decisions, she may need to adjust her explanations to address any biases he might have. But this doesn't change the need for her to separate her personal self from objectivity in her role.'

'If Nancy is going to be successful as a manager, I think it's very important for her to learn to recognize the difference between her personal, subjective arguments and what is actually an objective view.'

'I believe Nancy needs to learn to control her emotions, learn at every opportunity and become brave enough to be flexible in accepting any solution if it is the one that creates value.'

## 2. Stand behind the decisions you make.

'I believe that ego, when understood as self-esteem, is very much needed in sound decision-making. People's self-esteem can be a lever for creativity, innovation, willingness to change, communication and collaboration. By contrast, low self-esteem inhibits reflection, and thus leads to lower overall quality of decision-making.'

'It is not possible to be totally objective in decision-making, or to keep ego completely out of it.'

'An important factor in bringing your 'thinking' to the fore is your own self-confidence. If you believe that it's okay to make unpopular decisions for the sake of long-term value, then you can be much more confident in making such decisions.'

'Nancy needs to develop more confidence in her own analysis and vision.'

## 3. 'Thinking' should have a basis.

'Sound decisions are made when you have a good understanding of the model of how the business works. You need to be a student of your business, understand how the money is made, and what your competitive advantages are. So what I 'think' needs to be built on a foundation of data and business understanding.'

'Thinking is not the same as merely believing what your gut tells you, and shouldn't be. When I say I rely on what I 'think', I mean that I try to reflect on past experiences and skills as a means of effectively addressing new situations.'

'Though data cannot replace 'thinking', it can certainly improve it.'

## Our Thoughts

Nancy stands at a crossroads. Whether she recognizes it or not, Calvin has given both her and Dana a clear message about his priorities, and at this point she had better listen. He has said, in no uncertain terms, that he wants both of them to put all of their energy, intelligence and resourcefulness into creating long-term value for The Tipton Group, with no exception and no deviation.

Nancy (and Dana) should be thankful that they have received an unambiguous message from a candid boss. Straightforward messages leave no room for confusion or interpretation. In his direct words to Nancy and Dana, Calvin is deliberately reflecting the kind of approach he is asking them to take with regard to their decisions. He is telling them both, with no vagueness to speak of, that his aim regarding the two of them is to maximize the potential value they bring to the table as individuals and as collaborators. In so doing, he is also telling them that this is the way in which he wants them to approach their work – from a standpoint of value, nothing else.

Nancy is feeling nervous and fragile around Dana, and, to a lesser degree, around Calvin, too. She has exposed her feelings in the e-mail to Calvin about Dana, and now, after this discussion, and having received no response from Calvin to the e-mail, may regret having put those feelings to words. Nancy probably feels, rightly so, that the just-concluded meeting was in part Calvin's way of saying, 'Don't bother me with e-mails about someone you feel is not being nice to you'. He has made it clear that they must share a common objective. He has also made it very clear, without saying so explicitly, that there will be no room for individuals in this role who cannot adopt a shared view.

So what is Nancy to do? She needs to go back to her desk, think hard about what Calvin has said, and really try to absorb his words before jumping back into work. She must try to avoid internal reactions like, 'I can't believe he would say that', 'Why didn't he reprimand Dana for the way she treats me?' or 'How can I work effectively with someone like that?' She needs to remind herself that not everyone is going to mirror her own personality and behaviour, and that, in the end, companies thrive – or at least *can* thrive – on the diversity of their people and the different abilities and backgrounds they represent.

This will not be easy for Nancy, because we have seen to date that her natural reflex is more often an emotional one than a professional one. Such reactions would have remained largely concealed in her previous role at Whitesands, where interaction with others at a senior level was infrequent and she herself had a more junior, more functionally focused, role to fulfil. Her position now demands a much more resilient, business-focused approach. Perhaps she is, in some ways, regretting her promotion, and would find it easier to return to her old, 'comfortable' role in which she didn't have to deal with such issues on such a transparent level. This may indeed be an issue of self-esteem.

It would be tremendously helpful for Nancy to reach out to a potential mentor, or someone in her personal network, to help focus her down the path Calvin is so definitely asking her to follow. She cannot influence Dana's perspective or behaviours or, for that matter, anyone else's. But she can control her own. She should pick up the phone, invite Dana for lunch, and go forward.

**Your Thoughts**

## HUGO

### The Scenario

*Earlier in the week, Hugo spontaneously engaged his boss Dino in a dia-logue about the multiple and varied opinions being expressed by the mem-bers of his marketing team. He felt intimidated by the strength and convic-tion of their views and, moreover, his ability to reconcile them. Dino talked to Hugo about the need to stress collective objectivity and fairness in all matters as a critical element in value creation. Opinions, he said, have no place in such an effort, and he urged Hugo to make clear to his team that, while knowledge, experience and insight can be important contributors to value, in the end, only data and objectivity truly matter.*

*Hugo is working at his desk when he hears, 'Hey, Big H!' He looks up to see Peter Falkenberg, VP Asia, bursting into his office like a hurricane. Here's how the rest of their conversation proceeds.*

HUGO:    Peter. Hi. I didn't know you were still in the office.

PETER:   I just wanted to say hey. I'm heading back to Hong Kong in an hour. It was great to gab with you earlier.

HUGO:    Likewise. I hope it was a productive trip.

PETER:   Definitely got some things done. Just finished yakking with Dino about the rollout of that new line of stuffed animals. Stuffed ani-mals! I'll tell you one thing: I never saw a teddy bear at my old job.

HUGO:    Yeah. I think the designs are cute, but I wonder whether kids will take to them.

PETER:   Hm.

HUGO:    Something wrong?

PETER:   Nope.

HUGO:    Are you sure?

PETER:   Ah, listen, I don't want to flap my lips just to hear myself talk. It's all good.

HUGO:    No, it's all right. Please – tell me what's on your mind. I think you have something you want to say. I'm always happy to receive input from colleagues.

PETER: Okay. It's just that you just started that sentence with 'I think …'

HUGO: I did?

PETER: Yeah. Look, I'm not the kinda guy who goes around telling other people how to do things. Forget I said anything. Have a good one. I'll catch you in a few weeks.

*(Peter starts to leave. Hugo stands up.)*

HUGO: Peter, wait.

*(Peter stops and turns.)*

HUGO: Let me be clear here. I am happy to hear your thoughts. My ego is not in this room, okay? I am not going to be offended by what you say. I'm happy to listen, and then I reserve the right to adopt or dismiss what you say. Does that sound fair?

*(Peter sits back down. So does Hugo.)*

PETER: Man, you have a serious noggin there, Big H. Okay, the truth is I get a bit worried when anyone starts saying 'I think' this and 'I think' that. I mean, look, I don't trust a single thought I have.

HUGO: You don't?

PETER: No, sir, I do not.

HUGO: Why not?

PETER: Because it doesn't make a damn bit of difference what I think! The only thing that makes a difference is if I can help bring value to this company, and if I can teach the people below me in the org chart the same thing.

HUGO: I'm a bit confused. If you know what you're talking about and you have the right answers, what's wrong with saying, 'I think' as a starting point?

PETER: Depends why you're saying it. If you're saying it because you care if people agree with you or not, that might be a problem, because then you might start making decisions based on what other people might agree with, or you might start decid-ing what you think because of what you think other people want you to think. See what I mean?

HUGO: I don't think so.

PETER: Good one.

HUGO: It wasn't supposed to be a joke.

PETER: Good one anyway. Okay – if you're saying 'I think' without anything behind it, that's one thing. Like if you've got nothing but the thought, meaning your own opinion. But if you're saying 'I think' to mean, you know, 'This is what I think the info is telling us', well, now we're talking about something pretty different.

HUGO: So what do you say when you have to give someone on your team specific direction?

PETER: I try to make the case without talking about what I think. I say, look, here's the analysis, and here's what I see in it. Do you see it, too? I ask as many questions as I can, even when I believe I have the answer. I try to get other people to help me see the info through their eyes, because that can open up new lenses. I'm pretty good at what I do, but I miss stuff. I miss stuff all the time. No one has the crystal ball, so it's up to all of us to look at the same thing but in different ways. Know what I mean?

HUGO: Strangely, I think I do.

PETER: Ah, listen, what the hell do I know? I just wanted to drop in before I take off.

HUGO: I think you know a lot. Thanks.

*(Hugo raises his fist for a fist-bump. Peter, smiling, gives it to him.)*

## Questions We Asked

1. How would you interpret what Peter is saying to Hugo?
2. In your role, how much do you rely on what you 'think'?
3. Think of the leaders in your organization. When they need to give others direction, do they do it mostly with opinion and persuasion or data and information? Which approach is more effective? Why?

## Comments We Got

As a group, our participants seemed to divide into a few different ways of interpreting Peter's message to Hugo. One camp took a highly literal view, asserting that nothing matters beyond hard data and that there is no other discussion to be had. Another group argued that the best decisions result from a combination of data and 'thinking', with a general consensus that 'thinking' means the accumulation of relevant knowledge and experience brought to the situation by all of the various parties involved, or context-specific elements like scope, external influences and audience. Finally, a selection of the participant group conceded that, despite their organization's best efforts to endorse applicable data and objective analyses as the appropriate means by which to make value-based decisions, it is not uncommon for 'thinking' – often, the thinking of those at the top, or of the majority – to supersede, or at least significantly influence, important decisions.

Three themes surfaced out of the community's general responses. Here they are, including some of the most pertinent comments.

**1. 'Take 'thinking' out of decisions ...**

'Peter is saying all you should care about are hard facts and objective analyses. He's right.'

'Peter isn't comfortable with people making decisions based solely on opinions. And "I think the toys are cute" is an opinion.'

'I try to spend a great deal of time making sure that I understand the data that drives our business. If we have to make a decision without all of the relevant data, we try to make it from a basis built on as much data as is available.'

'Peter is bringing objective reasoning to his approach; Hugo appreciates that.'

**2. ... at least, to the extent it's possible ...**

'Data are very important, combined with strong experience. I'm not sure that being completely data-based is possible.'

'In my organization and, I believe, in most big organizations, decisions tend to be made based on the rule of the majority – that is, what the most people "think".'

'I rely on "thinking" quite a bit in my role. While I try as much as possible to rely on past situations and experience to base my thinking process and to articulate recommendations, it is not always helpful in resolving issues!'

'Data and information have power, and we think we should base our direction most of the case. However, sometimes, especially at the critical decision at the critical moment, top management with strong opinion prevails.'

**3. ... and recognize that other sources can help with the decision.**

'In my business, we tend to be very data-based. However, there is often discussion with the people closer to the action to ensure that something important and relevant is not being missed before a decision is made.'

'We all feel the pressure to make decisions. One of my best sources is how people in the field are "feeling" about a potential decision. Their experience can be invaluable; I use it as a check for my own understanding of a given situation.'

'The methods used by senior leadership in my organization depend on context, audience and the specific circumstances. The more tangible the matter, the more data and information they use. By contrast, when launching our enterprise social network, which heavily involved cultural and behavioural change, the company leaders expressed strong opinions and used overt persuasion, trying to use emotion to create consensus around the change.'

## Our Thoughts

Though Hugo and Peter are virtual opposites, we imagine that Hugo is thankful for Peter as a counterpart, and that the reverse is likely true as well. We have seen a consistent sense of openness and curiosity from Hugo throughout the beginning of his GM journey, and Peter seems to appreciate a similar give-and-take. While Hugo continues to exhibit a general diffidence, his confidence seems to be slowly growing – not because he is more assertive or demanding, but because he continues to ask questions and is committed to getting the most out of the answers. Hugo recognizes that others have valuable experience to share, and that even someone like Peter, though he may come off as a blowhard at first, can be enormously helpful in teaching Hugo how to be an effective general manager.

Hugo is putting himself in a more favourable position than, as a direct example, Nancy, who is allowing personal emotions to get in the way of making sensible decisions because she has not yet adopted a firm viewpoint based on value creation. Note that we said Hugo is *putting himself* in a more favourable position. This does not mean he is cleverly orchestrating situations to elevate his status, manipulating conversations to sway people to his side, or strategically manoeuvring through political minefields. His progress is resulting from a much simpler mental and practical shift than that. He has internalized, with full dedication and commitment, Dino's original message about staying focused on value, and he is using this message as the foundation for all of his decisions – including the decision to seek regular guidance from his boss, the decision to communicate a consistent set of objectives and a strict data focus to his team, the decision to befriend the numbers and get smart about concepts like the Discounted Expected Free Cash Flows, and the decision to invite ongoing feedback from trusted colleagues, like his opposite number Peter.

**Your Thoughts**

\* \* \*

## Overall Discussion

Freddy, Nancy and Hugo have made varying progress in learning how to accept their new roles, managing different relationships with others, and remaining focused on value-based strategy. They have faced tests to their mental perspectives and their practical approaches. They have been forced to look at leadership in a vastly different way, and from a broader lens, than they ever had to in their previous functions.

Now, they have reached the point where they must not only hold others accountable to the sustainable value orientation, but they must turn the focus onto themselves as well. Each of our three GMs has spent a lot of time being encouraged by their bosses or peers to look at investment decisions with an objective eye and a future-looking compass. In this chapter, each has come to realize that the most important person to hold accountable to the value orientation is him- or herself. In dealing with the management team of the acquired company, Freddy must remind himself of his role and his purpose. Nancy, after having a tough meeting with Calvin, must make a pivotal decision on whether she will take his words as admonishing, and wilt from them, or inspiring, and use them to grow. Hugo, hearing hinted-at words from the outspoken Peter, must invite feedback wherever he can get it and remind himself that his willingness to learn, listen and ask questions will ultimately win out over his personal insecurity about the ability to execute.

It is a combination of the readiness to ask and listen and the commitment to stay focused on value that will put our GMs in increasingly good stead and allow them to be true contributors of value to the organization. They are, in a sense, learning *how* to learn, in a way that was not required in their prior incarnations. They are learning how to learn constantly, without allowing opinions – theirs, or anyone else's – to compromise their focus on sound, value-based decision-making. Before, our GMs provided input to a decision-making process overseen by someone else. Now, they have become important priority-makers, and it is their decisions that will be held up to scrutiny by parties on every side, above, below and across. To become truly successful leaders, they must embrace, and maximize, their own individual journey, which will in turn allow them to complete the transformation into true creators of value for their organizations.

To understand the concept of value is one thing. To learn the practical tools for estimating and measuring it properly is another. To embed it simultaneously as a frame of mind and an operative approach is the final hurdle. As our GMs will learn, one can continually propel value and drive sustainable success only by seeking relevant data, using sound finance techniques, asking the right questions of the right people at the right time and listening to their bias-free input, keeping others focused on value-driven goals, maintaining fair process – and, above all, holding themselves and others answerable to an unflinching value-based perspective. It has become less about proving themselves to others as it has become about proving themselves to themselves.

## Key Questions to Ask Yourself

1. How much time do you typically devote to self-reflection and seeking to understand the extent to which your behaviours are driven by your personal agenda and emotional interests, as opposed to a value orientation on behalf of the organization?
2. How effectively are you able to separate substantive issues from personal/emotional issues as they pertain to your own work-related ambitions and feelings? Are you able to remain constructive and learning-oriented in the face of personal anxiety or emotional intensity?

3. Developing a subconscious ability to be data-driven requires considerable conscious effort (similar to conscious-level learning about how to drive a car, which eventually becomes subconscious-level ability). Are you aware of, and do you continuously challenge, your subconscious to remain data-driven and value-oriented?

# Chapter 8

## Passing the Test

### FREDDY

#### The Scenario

*A few days earlier, following his first merger meeting with the Chicago leadership, Freddy came to Trish to ask for advice. She had warned him about the difficult and sometimes emotion-filled conversations that he was going to encounter in his new role, but being warned about it and actually experiencing it first-hand proved very different. Those on the acquired side exhibited many different feelings and behaviours, from vulnerability to aggressiveness, and Freddy found himself ill-equipped to manage the interaction effectively. Sticking to his value orientation became more difficult when faced with this level of collective anxiety and frustration.*

*Trish encouraged him to remain focused and objective, but also to put himself in their shoes, so he could appreciate the position they find they are in and the kinds of reactions this might spark. She urged him to be empathetic as a means of understanding all perspectives at the table, but not sympathetic or catering to the emotions present, which would lead down the wrong road.*

*Freddy is working at his desk when he sees an e-mail from Trish appear in his Inbox. The only two recipients on the e-mail are him and Vivian Ho, his boss. The subject line of the e-mail is 'Reorg'.*

*Freddy pauses. Trish wants to talk to him and Vivian about reorganization? He wonders to himself whether this means reorganization on the Prism side, the side of the acquired company, or the new blended company. It makes sense to him that Trish would continue to involve him in a prominent role, but he is somewhat surprised that the invitation includes Vivian, who has thus far not played any significant role in the merger process.*

*Vivian is, of course, Freddy's superior. Until now, he has been focused mostly on managing the people below him and trying to create a productive dynamic with those on the merger team. He realizes he hasn't paid much thought to Vivian's role in this, because there hasn't really been one.*

*He begins to worry. Is Trish going to call out the fact that Freddy has not properly involved Vivian? Despite the fact that it has been Trish encouraging Freddy's participation and pushing him along, maybe she assumed that he would have been engaging his immediate supervisor automatically, all the while – which he has not. Freddy wonders whether, in not broadening his focus enough to keep in the loop the one person he should be, he has stumbled badly and alienated his own boss.*

*He thinks back over his recent conversations with Vivian and wonders whether, because of her vaguely curt comments and contradictory perspective on long-term value, he has unconsciously kept her at arm's length throughout the process. He recalls details of the recent meeting among him, Vivian and Trish in which he argued vehemently for a value-based perspective and a push for continual innovation, and the resistance both Trish and Vivian expressed in reply. The difference is that Trish has been flexible and open-minded, allowing Freddy to explore this perspective, inviting him to perform the analysis of the potential Midwest acquisition, and now look where he is. Vivian, on the other hand, has not budged an inch from that initial discussion, and in fact only seems to have become more disgruntled as Freddy's visibility and standing have risen.*

*Still, he wonders whether he has made a grave miscalculation, and just what is meant by Trish's subject line.*

*At the designated time, Freddy goes to Trish's office. Vivian arrives at the same time. Trish's door is closed, and they can see she's on the phone. Here's what takes place.*

FREDDY: Hi, Vivian.

VIVIAN: Good morning. Any idea what this is about?

FREDDY: She didn't tell me.

VIVIAN: I thought you knew everything these days.

FREDDY: What do you mean?

VIVIAN: Nothing. Just joking around.
*(The door opens.)*

TRISH: Hi, you two. Come on in and have a seat.
*(Freddy and Vivian sit.)*

TRISH: That was the boss. Before that, I spoke to the head of the merger team in Chicago. They want us to present a recommended organizational reconfiguration in a couple of weeks.

FREDDY: Reconfiguration?

TRISH: Essentially a new org chart, including which roles should stay, which should go, which should be combined or changed, and the projected benefits. We're going to work with HR to generate the recommendation.

VIVIAN: This is going to be a giant headache.

TRISH: There's more. My boss is asking that we present our recommendations in a … certain way.

FREDDY: What do you mean?

TRISH: I mean according to certain … inclinations.

VIVIAN: You're saying they want to make sure that the people from our side are put into the positions of power on their side.

TRISH: I didn't say that. But yes, you've got it.

FREDDY: And are we just going with that?

TRISH: Well, suffice to say, those above me have very specific ideas about how this should go, and while they obviously have the company's best interests at heart …

FREDDY: Do they?

VIVIAN: What are you saying, Freddy?

FREDDY:  If they're asking us to skew the recommendations to satisfy the
         … what was the word you used, Trish … 'inclinations' of specific
         individuals, is that what we call the company's best interests? If
         the goal of the acquisition is to gain knowledge of digital media,
         then we shouldn't be barreling in and blindly taking over. We
         should be letting the people who work there do what they do,
         and we should be watching and learning. We know very little
         about this space. The whole purpose of targeting this company
         in the first place was to extract the synergies and the deep
         knowledge they have.

VIVIAN:  Look, I'm sure they're just being appropriately cautious.

FREDDY:  So we aren't supposed to say what is actually in the best
         interests of the company, but instead say what they want us
         to say to protect the jobs or elevate the status of a handful of
         select people? This org chart is a crucial part of developing
         important knowledge. It needs to support that objective, not the
         biases of our executives.

TRISH:   We're going to have to strike a balance here, Freddy. I know it
         isn't the most desirable scenario to you, but there are people in
         certain positions who have certain ideas, and we can't change
         that.

FREDDY:  Maybe we can't change it entirely. But can we not try to
         encourage them to see what value creation is and what
         it isn't?

VIVIAN:  Look, Freddy, I know you want to change the world overnight,
         but it's a process. It's not as though the people who run this
         company don't know anything.

FREDDY:  I don't think I said anything like that.

VIVIAN:  Maybe not, but it certainly sounds like you're implying –

FREDDY:  I'm saying that you're describing missing the opportunity to real-
         ize the learning from this acquisition – which was the whole point
         of it – as 'appropriately cautious'.

VIVIAN:  I just think that you could manage to show a little more flexibility.
         You aren't quite CEO yet.

FREDDY:  What?

TRISH:     Okay, guys, this isn't helpful. Look, Freddy, I see your point, but there are political realities to deal with, as there are in any company. You have to understand that.

FREDDY:  Trish, do political realities mean suddenly undermining the whole objective because of the whims of a few people at the top?

VIVIAN:   No. It means sometimes you have to compromise.
           *(Trish doesn't say anything. Freddy doesn't say anything. Vivian doesn't say anything. Uncomfortable silence hangs in the air.)*

## Questions We Asked

1. What would you do in Freddy's position?
2. To what degree have you experienced a challenge to your integrity, being asked to put aside your view of the 'correct' behaviour to follow behaviour proposed by superiors? How did you deal with it?
3. Is Vivian rationalizing the compromise to herself to keep her career on track, or do you feel she really believes in management's request to present a biased analysis? Does it matter which she is doing?

## Comments We Got

To a person, our participants sympathized with Freddy's position, while at the same time encouraging him to think with a level head and tread with caution. People strongly shared the opinion that Vivian is in self-preservation mode and – seemingly – threatened by, or upset about Freddy's dogged focus on value creation and long-term goals at the expense of making what are, in her mind, reasonable short-term decisions – like kow-towing to the whims of Prism's senior leadership. Most suggested that Freddy continue to stand firm in his beliefs, at least to the point where those beliefs are truly and irretrievably in conflict with those who see things differently, at which point he would have to choose to either risk his job or quit and seek a role elsewhere which is better suited to his outlook.

The majority of participants felt that Freddy's main challenge is no longer in expressing his position or arguing clearly for a value orientation, but in determining just how far is too far when it comes to pushing these convictions amid the divergent perspectives among him, Trish and, in particular, Vivian. There is no formula, most agreed, and no easy answer. Every situation is different, and one must decide for himself where the appropriate line is that balances personal integrity, political security and organizational well-being. Freddy has an important decision to make, the group collectively agreed. And that decision, in the end, is up to him.

The participant community's overall responses reflected three connected themes. Here they are, along with representative comments.

## 1. Fight for what you think is right, but understand your role.

'I think Freddy needs to aim for a combination of firmness and flexibility. He must somehow creatively find a way to blend the view he believes in with what Trish is asking of him and Vivian. At the end of the day, Vivian is his superior, and so she gets to call the shots. He needs to respect the fact that she is responsible and accountable for him. If he really can't reconcile the two positions, he needs to be prepared to quit.'

'I would advise Freddy to stick to the original objective but only be as assertive as necessary. He's in a sticky spot, but I firmly believe his best approach is to remind Trish of the rationale behind his analyses and affirm that, in the long run, the actions they suggest are in the best interests of the company. The problem is that, having said this, if you are a member of the organization, you ultimately do have to follow the decision-making process and chain of command. You have a right to speak up and fight for what you believe in, but once the decision is made, you have to do your best to make it happen according to what those above you want, otherwise the organization will collapse.'

## 2. Stick to the data.

'Freddy's argument should start and end with data. Nothing else should be relevant. At this point he should take Trish deeper into his argument or analysis from a factual basis, highlighting in particular expected free cash flow projected from the acquisition. There is an estimate that the FCF is based on the company both continuing to operate and generate the cash flow as it had before, and likely, an additional stream that comes from making some synergy changes. He should offer to show Trish and her superiors his estimates of the impact of the acquired company's change in earnings if (a) it is left alone (no changes in leadership), (b) leadership is gutted and the owning company leadership installed or (c) a balanced approach is taken (one or two leadership positions changed with a likely minimal impact on earnings). Using this approach, he can keep Trish and the other senior leaders focused on what matters. It's all about the data.'

## 3. Everyone has their own idea of compromise.

'I face this kind of situation often. When having to compromise your beliefs, it isn't always easy to measure how far is "too far". If it goes beyond a certain degree, I think you have to be ready to leave the organization. I haven't reached that point yet, but it's fair to say that I've had to be "flexible" on a number of decisions because of what my superiors believed in contrast with what I felt.'

'I find myself in this kind of situation occasionally. When it happens, I try to build an argument involving different ways of achieving the goal, all of which align with the approach I believe in. If my argument falls on deaf ears, I try to ask for clarification of the rationale to behave in the requested way. I think it is a way of distancing myself from the sense of guilt.'

'This happens. It's happened to me more than once. The question is always the same: how do you decide when your behaviour is correct, or fair?'

'It seems like Vivian is convincing herself that she believes in what management is asking for the sake of career preservation. I understand the instinct to do this in the moment, but it is not a sustainable way of operating.'

'There are battles, and there are wars. Freddy needs to stay focused on winning the war. I can think of plenty of times I have sacrificed winning a battle to concentrate on the bigger, often longer-term objective. If losing the battle is estimated to be of minimal impact, I will just get on board. If the projected impact is big, I will fight, debate, cite data and try to make the case as best I can. If the idea of rolling over in the battle is totally asinine, the only choice is to be honest with my team and say: "Look, this is what we have to do because there are people above me who have more authority. I don't agree with it, but we have to focus on winning the war."'

'I think Vivian is obviously conflicted. Before entering the meeting, she clearly vents some frustration about Freddy "knowing everything these days", meaning she resents the fact that people are impressed by him. Then, during the meeting, she quite aggressively endorses the "biased" option – perhaps not entirely, but enough to suggest that Freddy should take a more balanced, less one-sided view. By doing so, she is aligning herself with Trish and thus accepting the dictates of senior management.'

'I think Vivian is rationalizing the compromise because she has a serious fear of rocking the boat. It is a contrast to Freddy's attitude – he is all about finding the right value solution for the organization.'

'It's a little disconcerting to hear Vivian willingly tossing aside her original justification for the merger for the purpose of being politically safe. She needs to remember that part of her job is making sure her leaders are aware of potentially value-destroying actions. This kind of behaviour can't last in the long run. Freddy might be putting himself in a riskier position, but if upper management is really focused on the survival of the company, they will thank and reward him for his contribution to long-term value.'

## Our Thoughts

One must make political decisions at work. They are avoidable only if one works for oneself, in which case the criteria for any decision involves the views of just one person, making the perspective narrower but the environment much simpler. Freddy has found an ally in Trish throughout this process, but now he is thrown for a loop when she tells him and Vivian that they must cater to the whims of the higher-ups, who want the merger to go a certain way. They seem to want to preserve the balance of power not only in Prism's favour, but also have specific levels of authority and influence tilted toward a select handful of people.

Freddy is naturally opposed to this – but worse, he now feels ambushed and undermined by Trish's backtracking, compounding the indignation he already feels from Vivian, which seems only to be increasing. Trish seems to have reverted to her earlier cautious, conservative stance; Vivian seems paranoid about doing anything but bowing to the desires of those at the top rungs of the ladder.

What is Freddy to do? Does he push harder for his stance, creating a dangerous him-against-them scenario but relying ultimately on the continuing support of upper management? This would seem a risky proposition, since it is upper management who are the ones passing down the direction, via Trish. Does Freddy then merely acquiesce to the orders coming down the ranks, possibly compromising the goal of value creation that he fought so hard for to this point? Does he argue for a middle-ground in an attempt to generate as much value as possible while still creating the appearance of 'giving in', at least to enough of an extent that he won't be seen as a mischief-maker?

There is no easy solution, nor is there a simple equation Freddy can apply to figure out what to do. He indeed has some big decisions to make. He knows the situation may be inflammatory if handled the wrong way. The question is, which way is 'wrong' and which is 'right'? As others mentioned in their comments, Freddy needs to assess for himself whether this is a 'battle' or the 'war' and, based on that determination, decide how hard he wishes to fight for the value perspective he believes in, as opposed to seeking a compromise wherein he does his best to reconcile competing objectives.

From our own experience, we would recommend doing a value assessment of his options. If Freddy chooses the compromise approach, he will be able to continue to build his reputation and his network in order to support the long-term value-creation objective. His main risk is that, in compromising, he may also compromise his integrity to a point where he is no longer willing to tolerate himself, in which case he should quit Prism.

An additional risk is that, by compromising, the perception of fairness that Freddy has worked hard to establish, and which is intrinsically linked to value creation in the human brain, may be undermined in the eyes of his peers, superiors or subordinates, who may then associate him with these unfair (i.e. non-value-based) decisions, in turn limiting his ability to lead and manage those people in the future. If Freddy chooses the path of compromise, he must minimize the potential damage while deriving maximum benefit to himself and for the organization. From a value perspective, if the upside can be preserved and the downside mitigated to make the net effect value-creating, Freddy will have chosen the right path.

---

**Your Thoughts**

## NANCY

### The Scenario

*It has been a few days since Calvin summoned Nancy and her colleague Dana to his office and assured them that they were both valuable assets to the organization, while at the same time encouraging them to focus more on value-based decisions and less on personal differences, real or perceived. He suggested, more assertively than usual, that both do their best to leverage each other's talents and skills and simultaneously leave opinions – and personal feelings – aside in deference to an ongoing focus on value creation and the decisions necessary to support it.*

*Nancy is now working at her desk when she hears a knock on her open office door. She looks up to see a smiling Dana. They have not had an interaction since the previous meeting with Calvin. Here's how the exchange proceeds.*

DANA:    Morning.

NANCY:   Hi, Dana.

DANA:    How's your day going?

NANCY:   Well, thanks. And you?

DANA:    Just fine, thanks for asking. Do you have a minute?

NANCY:   Yes, of course.

        *(Dana steps into Nancy's office.)*

DANA:    Do you mind if I close the door?

NANCY:   No, that's fine.

        *(Dana closes the door.)*

DANA:    So what did you think of Cal's little sermon yesterday?

NANCY:   I suppose he feels we're both taking the wrong perspective.

DANA:    Yeah, seems that way. I mean, do you agree? How do you think he got the impression that we're so at odds?

NANCY:   I don't know.

DANA:    I find it pretty curious.

NANCY:   What he said made sense to me.

DANA:    Which part? What was your main takeaway from what he said?

NANCY:    I believe he was telling us that he values our contributions individually and jointly, but that he's encouraging us to leverage each other while keeping our egos aside.

DANA:    Yeah? To me, it was more like he was telling us just to play nice. You didn't get that?

NANCY:    Well, again, this may be simply a matter of seeing things differently. I don't think there's only one way to perceive something, or that either of us needs to convince the other that there is.

DANA:    Is that what you think I'm trying to do? Convince you to see it my way?

NANCY:    Dana …

DANA:    Nancy, I did not come in here to try to convince you of anything. I was just interested in what you got out of the conversation. Listen, we're not in competition.

NANCY:    I know that. I mean, that's exactly what he was trying to convey. Don't you agree?

DANA:    I just said that.

NANCY:    So what are you asking me?

DANA:    I'm not asking you anything.

NANCY:    Then, not to be rude, but what are we talking about? I'm not sure I'm clear on what you want out of this conversation.

DANA:    I thought we were supposed to remove personal agendas.

NANCY:    Look, I need to get this report out the door by end of day. I'm not trying to be impolite, but it seems like we're going in circles a bit.

DANA:    Guess you're right. Okay, well, I'll see you this afternoon at the weekly meeting.

NANCY:    Great. Have a good afternoon.

DANA:    You, too.

        *(Dana opens the door and leaves Nancy's office. Nancy shakes her head and rolls her eyes, then returns to her report.)*

## Questions We Asked

1. Nancy appears to be getting increasingly frustrated in her interactions with Dana. Why do you think this is?
2. What do you think Nancy should do to make the most out of this relationship?

3. Do you think Nancy's key challenge is in understanding the concept of value, or understanding the need for personal change?

## Comments We Got

Our participants were not happy with Nancy following this scenario. They felt that she had been given opportunity after opportunity to place her ego aside, rise above her emotions, establish more professional behaviour, demonstrate a stronger focus on the business, and seek ways to maximize the relationship with Dana, and that she is failing at all of them. Everyone seemed to agree that Dana's purpose for striking up this conversation with Nancy was to mend fences and move forward, as Calvin suggested, but that Nancy once again derailed any possibility of reconciliation based on a big reaction to a small comment.

While none of our participants are particular fans of Dana, nor would any of them welcome the scenario in which they had to work with her, they were, interestingly, even less impressed with Nancy. For all her behavioural faults, Dana is at least focused, in every conversation, on the working relationship and the business at hand. Her priority, despite her ill manner, is Tipton itself. The group did not feel the same about Nancy, who seems to divert every conversation, somehow dragging it down into a standoff of personal contrasts, causing mutual frustration between her and Dana and creating an ongoing impasse between the two.

The majority of comments about Nancy came off like those of parents at their wits' end in trying to figure out how to change the behaviours of a problem child. Indeed, it is Nancy's childlike behaviour that people see as the continuing problem. They agree that, like a child, she is having tremendous difficulty expanding her focus, not taking words personally and thinking from a sufficiently broad perspective. Almost all of our participants' continued to urge her to change her ways, and continue to be frustrated with her for refusing to do so.

Two distinct themes came out of the overall responses received. Here they are, with specific comments highlighted.

## 1. You can't contribute value if you're focused on yourself.

'It seems Nancy is still angry about being insulted by Dana, and can't leave it behind. It's a highly counterproductive way to go about things.'

'Nancy doesn't seem to be able to deal with emotions easily. She's still carrying forth her resentment toward Dana from previous conversations.'

'Nancy is showing a great deal of ambivalence. She understands the situation and articulates it well, but doesn't seem able to make the effort to meet in the middle, or make any movement toward Dana's side.'

'Nancy gives the impression of false calm, but her real emotions are transparent. She has to learn to get past this.'

'Nancy needs to change her ways, otherwise she is just not going to last in this, or any, company. It isn't that she doesn't understand value; it's that she can't seem to let go of her self-focus and personal baggage. She's far too focused on people's opinions of her, and she obviously lets those opinions affect her perspective. She needs to learn not to wear her frustrations so prominently on her suit – even if she thinks she's hiding them!'

'Nancy is probably feeling a little attacked by Dana, who is a bit relentless in her way. She's also probably feeling somewhat guilty for having sent the e-mail which led to the meeting with Calvin in the first place.'

## 2. Don't focus on winning. Focus on maximizing relationships.

'Nancy is trying to manipulate the situation by lying to Dana, saying, 'Why do you think Calvin had that conversation with us?' Nothing good can come of such devious practices. She needs to just lay her cards on the table with Dana and figure out how they can match their contrasting styles to the maximum value benefit of the company.'

'At this point, I think Nancy needs to minimize her interface with Dana. She isn't getting anything from her, and she doesn't seem able to strike any kind of compromise between the two styles.'

'I think Nancy's best move would be to take the opportunity offered by Dana to talk. After all, Dana is making the effort to come to see her to try to find 'a way to work together' so that their individual and joint contribution can be rewarded/appreciated. Nancy would do herself a favour if she could find it in herself to make a move toward Dana and compromise on some of her positions. With that as a starting point, there will probably be the opportunity to later bring Dana slowly to her position – if that is truly the most valuable direction.'

'Some way, somehow, Nancy has got to put aside her ego. Her best option is to spend some time with Dana, focusing on getting to know her better, and thus be able to work with her better. Nancy might even admit that she sent Calvin the e-mail that prompted the mess, to clear the deck, start fresh and reach out to get things moving in the right direction again.'

'If Nancy could just manage to step outside herself, she would benefit greatly. She seems incredibly resistant to the prospect of personal change. She needs to look in the mirror and remind herself that any learning is good, regardless from whom you learn it.'

'Nancy is forcing herself to keep Dana at arm's length. It also seems important to her to be the one who understands things 'better'. Her quiet condescension and hostility is not helping the situation one iota. Dana's approach is not exactly the right one, but at least it's real.'

## Our Thoughts

Nancy's main issue is not that she is in a precarious position, but that she does not seem to recognize it. The two approaches she is taking with Dana at the moment, avoidance and confrontation, will not hold up over time. Calvin is too savvy a boss not to see these behaviours, and Dana is likely too clever not to do something more definitive after enough rebuffed attempts at reconciling.

If Nancy cannot identify her shortfalls and do something about them quickly, she is in serious trouble. It is true that she has started to change her thinking – slightly – about the import of a value orientation, and that she has started to consider more effective, consistent ways of managing communication with those on her team around this standpoint. What she seems to be willfully resisting, however, is the necessity to remove *herself* – her feelings, her reactions, her perceptions, her reputation – from the greater goal of contributing value to the organization and reaping the benefits that could go along with accomplishment of that goal. She is entering every dialogue with Dana prepared for battle, instead of aiming at a common solution and a foundation from which to move forward productively as colleagues.

The successful transition to general management involves several tests of one's leadership. Some of them are mental or intellectual. Others are practical or behavioural. The most important one is personal. Nancy must figure out a way to pass that test. If she can't, she is going to find the window of opportunity on her new role closing, and fast.

**Your Thoughts**

# HUGO

## The Scenario

*The previous day, Hugo's energetic colleague and counterpart in Asia, Peter Falkenberg, burst into his office to say goodbye before returning to his home office. At a certain point in the conversation, Hugo offered an opinion about the new line of teddy bears being rolled out by AMR, and Peter paused. After Hugo asked him to share what he was thinking, Peter echoed the thoughts offered earlier by Hugo's boss Dino about the danger of opinions. Peter kindly cautioned Hugo about saying 'I think …' as a means either of giving an opinion not backed by data or of responding to the opinions of others. In any given scenario, Peter suggested, one has to diligently monitor one's own instincts so that opinion-giving is minimized and true contribution to value-creation decisions maximized.*

*Hugo is now in his office, at his computer, looking a bit tense. He is in the midst of composing an e-mail to his Marketing team.*

*As he types, he reads the words aloud to himself: '… the new line of stuffed animals promises to deliver incremental revenue of …'*

*Hugo pauses. 'Wait,' he says to himself. 'Do my guys really care about the revenue projections? We're a marketing team. It's about the experience that consumers will have with the stuffed animals as a product. That's what represents value to them, right? Right. At least I think that's right. Okay …'*

*Hugo keeps typing, and continues saying the words to himself: '… the new line of premium stuffed animals will offer a combination of quality and craftsmanship for which our research indicates there is a strong and receptive market segment …'*

*He pauses again, getting a little more frustrated. 'That isn't it, either,' he says. 'Damn.'*

*Finally, Hugo picks up the phone and dials Dino's extension. Dino answers. Here's how their conversation proceeds.*

DINO:  Hi, Hugo.

HUGO:  Hey, Dino. Listen, could I pick your brain about some stuff?

DINO:  Can you give me the short version? I'm pretty swamped at the moment.

HUGO:  Yes, of course.

*(Hugo pauses, then continues.)*

I feel like I'm taking one step forward and two steps back, and I could use your advice.

DINO:  Can you be a little more specific?

HUGO:  I buy the value message. Intellectually I understand the big picture and our need to point the company in the right direction by making sound decisions. I'm on board with that. The thing is, even though I get it, I feel like I'm not communicating it very well, or very consistently, either with my own team or the executive team.

DINO:  What's making you think that?

HUGO:  I feel like I don't know how to be with either side. As an example, I was just starting to type an e-mail to my group, trying to frame the new stuffed animal initiative within that overall message, and ... I don't know, I just don't think I'm getting it right. If it were me reading the e-mail, I wouldn't know what I was talking about. That's where I could use the help.

DINO:  I hear you loud and clear, Hugo. Understanding things intellectually doesn't mean you can make the personal change overnight. That takes some work. Listen, I have to keep my head down for the rest of the day, but how about you swing by my office tomorrow morning and we can start to talk it through?

HUGO:  Sure.

DINO:  All right. Speak to you later.

HUGO:  Bye. Thanks.

*(Hugo hangs up the phone, stares at his computer screen again, and sighs.)*

## Questions We Asked

1. What do you see as Hugo's primary struggle?
2. Have you ever known what to do but not known how to get yourself to do it, or how to get others to understand what you think they should be doing?
3. If you were Dino, what advice would you give Hugo?

## Comments We Got

Our participant group continues to pull for Hugo, for the same key reasons as before: he wants to do well, and he exhibits no ego. People agree that, while his confidence is rising in baby steps, it obviously still requires a big boost in order for him to communicate clearly, confidently and eloquently, as a successful manager must. Many suggested that Hugo could benefit from expanding his perspective when it comes to communicating with those on his team: focusing on the big value picture as a starting point, then funnelling the message down, or trying to integrate specific messages – in this case, the one about the new line of stuffed animals – into the overall objective of value creation for AMR as an organization.

Most also felt that he should, as a default position, ensure that he is communicating *something* to the team, even when he is not fully confident in what he is communicating. In the participant group's collective view, the need for Hugo to maintain his leadership visibility and transparency is high, and doing so will help him build increasing confidence as he continues to evolve in his managerial role. The team, most agreed, needs to know primarily that he is there at the leadership helm, and showing full conviction in his role. His message, and his style, will become finer and more sophisticated as his confidence and experience grows.

Four themes emerged from the overall responses to the current scenario. Here they are, along with representative comments.

## 1. Communicate dynamically.

'To me, Hugo's main struggle is twofold. First, finding the right level of integration between his ingrained marketing perspective and the larger, company-wide value perspective. And second, communicating it to his staff.'

'Hugo should put himself in the shoes of his group and think about what's going to get them excited about the value of this initiative. It's not easy, but thinking about a couple of group meetings or discussions to forget about the simple matter of the bears for a period of time might help. He should first concentrate on getting theoretical about value, so that they understand the true objectives, and then he should start making the connections to the bear launch. I don't think it's something to be done via e-mail. He should get into the habit of, when needing to communicate things that are going to be hard to understand, difficult to hear or potentially confusing, always trying to do it in person, or maybe by telephone or video chat if necessary. E-mail is just too impersonal. And he is a leader now.'

'Hugo seems to have a big struggle articulating the difference between value for a specific group of people (in this case, marketing) and the idea of ultimate absolute value from the company's perspective – that is, a common understanding of value regardless of roles, positions or departments. I think this is an area of critical learning and development for him to become a successful general manager.'

'I think Hugo's main issue is learning how to effectively communicate the need for the team to think about value. In this situation, he needs to tie the overall concept of value to the specific task at hand, which is getting the marketing people geared up to promote and launch the new line of teddy bears. The kinds of things he's talking about in his e-mail have mostly to do with why they should be excited about the bears, but it's not especially inspiring, nor is it a particularly good example of communicating value to the team.'

## 2. Your message should be about creating value.

'I think Hugo needs to keeps things simple, direct and as basic as possible. He needs to learn not to put everything up front that he thinks is relevant. He should present it simply, step by step, so that people can digest it without being confused or surprised. This will serve him especially well since he is a new authority figure to them. They will perceive the communication as to-the-point and goal-oriented.'

'If I were Dino, I would advise Hugo to lay things out as directly as possible for the team. Touch on the problem briefly, but focus on the potential solutions. Be succinct, clear and assertive about what he expects from the team.'

'In his communication, Hugo should clarify the ultimate goal as it pertains to expected value, and should talk about the justification in tangible terms. He should be very clear about the roles, contributions and expectations of the team and how they relate to the collective effort to achieve this goal.'

## 3. Feeling a bit lost isn't unusual.

'To me, Hugo has an issue with self-confidence. I think he understands value as Dino has explained it to him, but it seems he's very intimidated by the new position he finds himself in, and I think that this is coming through in his attempts to communicate with everyone around him. He needs to take the bull by the horns and embrace the authority he has, even if he isn't always going to say or write the perfect thing.'

'I find that, in this kind of instance, it's often important to just start with something – anything, not necessarily the most important or mission-critical aspect of a role or business. Hugo is trying, which is great, but I think he needs to push himself a little harder to realize that he can do this.'

'I think Hugo's struggle is a common one for a general manager, in particular during the initiation phase, where goals and objectives are clear but the path to reach them are not necessarily well defined, and therefore often unclear or unknown.

When taking a new position in a new environment, we can understand our role and know our responsibilities on paper, but it's a very different thing to fully master the techniques or processes that are necessary to fulfil them.'

### 4. Leverage others.

'Hugo is doing the right thing reaching out to Dino for help. I think this shows evidence that he can be a good leader – he is not pretending to know everything or to be able to handle his new transition seamlessly. I think he should try to do even more of this type of thing, enlisting as much expertise as he can from others to help himself on-board into the new role as effectively as he can.'

'Starting a new job is a lot about "drinking from the fire hose", and it appears Hugo is affected by this common syndrome. He has a lot to learn in a short period of time, and with such a flood of information it gets hard to step back and see the forest for the trees. Hugo is trying to figure out what to do with the new information Dino has given him, which is a good thing. I think he is acting appropriately by making the phone call.'

'When climbing a big learning curve quickly, it's always a positive step to ask for help from willing colleagues who have more experience, and therefore a better sense of where and how to start. This is where it's good that Hugo is seeking a little coaching from Dino.'

## Our Thoughts

In following Dino's original advice to cast aside everything he knows and abandon everything he brought to his previous role, Hugo now finds himself struggling to find the means to fulfil his *current* role. He feels he is caught in a 'one step forward, two steps back' pattern, whereby he learns or absorbs one important lesson only to fail to put it into practice because of his deficient managerial toolkit.

What all of you recognize, even if Hugo himself doesn't quite know it yet, is that in this blank-slate position he feels himself in, he is disposed well for success. Whether Hugo has strong inborn leadership 'stuff' – confidence, articulacy, intellect – is less important than his willingness to embrace the necessary leadership transformation that he knows he will need in order to be successful in this role.

In a sense, his lack of confidence works to his continuous advantage, because he does not possess the arrogance to think that he has all the answers or the skills to succeed without changing. He has let down his guard with Dino from the first conversation and discarded any resistance to growth. He has asked lots of questions and listened hard to the answers. He has admitted to feeling confused or lost and has solicited guidance and direction on a more or less constant basis about everything from practical finance tools to effective communication techniques. He has invested time and energy thinking about how to fulfil this role well and, ultimately, how to become the facilitator of value that Dino is encouraging him to be.

Though he remains dubious about his natural abilities and overall experience, Hugo does have one unalterable item in his toolbox that will continue to position him well on this journey: self-awareness. He acknowledges the passage he is making, has no illusions about its challenges and makes no assumptions about how quickly he will get there. Because of that, we are willing to bet that he will get there faster than he thinks.

**Your Thoughts**

\*   \*   \*

## Overall Discussion

Each of our GMs has tried in his or her own way to understand, internalize and implement a value orientation. All three now face the stark reality that their leadership journey involves much more than just absorbing a new message; it also involves adhering to that message even amid ongoing uncertainty, competing influences and, sometimes, express conflict.

In Freddy's case, that conflict is coming from a direction from senior management that stands at odds with his mindset and beliefs; in Nancy's case, from a stubborn self-focus and mulish resistance to change, compounded by her personal belief that the problem is a colleague she feels may prove her ultimate undoing; and in Hugo's case, from his own internal professional struggle and personal insecurity as he tries to balance the overall value message with specific tactical communications to his team. Each of the three must now consider their individual priorities in the context of the larger company objective. Their mettle is being put to the test as they weigh potentially convenient decisions and actions against more challenging and demanding ones that uphold the value orientation they have come to embrace.

Amid these competing pressures, the effort of maintaining the course they are on and justifying to others the importance of an ongoing value stance may at times feel to our GMs nothing short of exhausting, or simply not worth it. They have, to varying degrees and in different ways, shed old habits and adopted new ones. They have, in contrasting extents, espoused an objective, data-driven outlook and placed opinions aside. They have tried to cultivate an environment where feedback is given, information gathered and conclusions made. But now they must do something harder yet. Competing commitments, hidden assumptions and a number of powerful human tendencies can derail our attempts to change. Our GMs must not only be able to recognize these potential derailers; they must also be able to overcome them.

They are also coming to see that even their smallest decisions now have key implications for the business, and every move they make is going to fall under intense scrutiny from above, below, laterally, or all three. In addition, they may encounter surprising resistance from parties who they expected ought to support them most, whether senior leaders, peer executives or direct reports. Sometimes, the resistance will feel personal. At other times, it will seem as though others just don't get the overall value-creation message they are trying to communicate. Both have the power to cause deep frustration.

To confront this challenge, our GMs will need to look in the mirror and understand that the resistance is not about them, but about traditional short-term or narrow thinking and the consequent aversion to adopting an approach based on an intangible idea and a long-term orientation. They will need to figure out how to stay personally and emotionally detached while remaining staunch advocates of the right way of doing business. To accomplish this, they will need to apply specific tools that take the understanding they have now arrived at and make it achievable in their day-to-day reality. Models of human behaviour tell us that a number of instinctive behaviours will rear their heads and try to prevent this transformation. Our GMs have come to understand the necessity for their own mental and practical transformation. Now, they are fielding challenges to that transformation from all sides – most notably, from within.

## Key Questions to Ask Yourself

1. Are you sufficiently aware of your emotions and personal opinions to be able to step back from them when at work to ensure they don't dictate your reactions to others? When you are managing your emotions, is it simply an external veneer which, hopefully, prevents others from seeing your emotional responses, or are you honestly and successfully managing them in order to maintain a data-driven and value-oriented approach to managing your organization and your relationships?

2. When your personal views are inconsistent with the role/ decisions/approach you are required to take within your organization, are you able to put your views aside and play your role as a responsible member of the team? If not, are you prepared to quit in order to honour your personal views?

3. What guide do you employ to assess whether your behaviour is fair in the way it represents your personal agenda and/or your perception of the best behaviour for the long-term value of the organization? How effectively do you seek, and listen to, external counsel (spouse, friend, coworker distant from the situation, mentor, coach, etc.)?

# Chapter 9

---

# Sustaining the Journey

## FREDDY

### The Scenario

*The day before, Trish invited Freddy and his boss Vivian to a meeting in her office. Freddy was met with another passive-aggressive comment from Vivian just before entering Trish's office. Trish told Vivian and Freddy that senior management has asked that they provide a recommendation for how the company should be restructured in the coming post-merger months, including which of the acquired personnel and functions to absorb or eliminate, along with the projected benefits.*

*Trish added something surprising and significant: leadership wants them to bias these recommendations so that Prism executives stand to benefit most and remain most protected, regardless of the expected impact on long-term value. Vivian immediately endorsed leadership's stance, stating that they are exercising reasonable caution. Trish, until now aligned with Freddy's value orientation, seemed to revert, not wanting to push directly against management's stance.*

*When Freddy argued vigorously against accepting management's direction, Trish tried to talk him down, reminding him that company politics, the need to compromise and the power structure are realities, and it isn't logical to try to shake those to the core overnight. Freddy left Trish's office distressed and frustrated.*

*Now, Freddy is sitting at his desk. He has opened a new e-mail window and typed Trish's name in the recipient field. In the subject line, he types the words, 'Following up on our discussion of yesterday'.*

*Then he deletes the words and types just, 'Following up'. After a moment, he deletes those words as well. He stares at the blank field for a few seconds, then types, 'Thanks'.*

*He tabs down to the body of the e-mail, pauses, then begins to write. These are the words that appear across Freddy's screen, which he says aloud to himself as he types:*

> Dear Trish. Thanks for the conversation yesterday. I know I got a little heated, and I wanted to clarify my thoughts so you'll have the right perspective on them.
>
> I am very happy to have been given the opportunity to make a meaningful contribution to the new strategy. You asked me to step out of my comfort zone and challenged me to articulate why I felt a more thorough and objective analysis of the Midwest opportunity was needed, and I thank you for that. I felt intimidated being asked to actually prepare that analysis, but I'm very glad that you gave me the chance to do so. It has led to my being actively involved in an important initiative for the organization at a critical time. I am grateful to be able to offer whatever value I can in this respect.
>
> That said, in our meeting yesterday, I felt as though you were asking me to retreat again. I realize that there are politics to deal with and that the world can't be changed overnight, but I believe it is abundantly clear that Prism's traditional model isn't working, and I feel that, if decisions continue to be made the same way they were made before, we will continue to lose ground in the marketplace, and ultimately we will not be here any longer to even have these discussions. In the end, my authority and influence are pretty limited, so I guess I'm asking if we can discuss ways to put up a collective front and do everything possible to point the company in a direction that will lead to long-term success. I believe that would be in the best interests of all of us.
>
> Thanks for listening,
>
> Freddy

## Questions We Asked

1. Do you think sending this e-mail is a good move for Freddy?
2. Would you have said anything different, or differently?
3. How do you think Trish will respond?

## Comments We Got

Though to this point our participants have supported virtually all of Freddy's actions and decisions, their collective response to his sending this e-mail to Trish is that he has, for the first time, blundered. Most people felt that the e-mail, though well composed, represented an imprudent move, and one that, for the first time, showed Freddy letting his personal emotions get in the way. They also felt that Freddy's general approach to the situation was ill-considered and that, if anything, he should have raised the issue in person with Trish, not through an electronic message.

The participant community felt also, for the first time, that Freddy was acting from a narrow perspective instead of a broad one. His sending the e-mail, many suggested, was an act of extreme shortsightedness and an inward-facing mentality. Many noted that Freddy was acting out of frustration and a not-fully-thought-through sense of urgency, and that Trish would likely not receive this e-mail positively, since it largely ignores the message she has already delivered in a fairly clear manner: that it is her preference to unquestioningly carry out upper management's direction, whether or not it may represent a true and complete value orientation.

The majority of participants believe Freddy has dug himself a hole in sending this message to Trish – and almost everyone wondered how he is going to navigate his way out.

Three general themes stood out from the overall responses we received. Here they are, with comments included.

### 1. Don't communicate at arm's length.

'Things like this should never be e-mailed! They can be misconstrued, taken out of context, forwarded when you don't want them to be and so on. It isn't that I think Freddy's thoughts aren't sound, or that his concerns aren't legitimate. But I think he needs to be a little more thoughtful about what Trish might do with it.'

'I don't think this kind of e-mail is going to get Freddy anywhere with Trish. If anything, I think it would make her feel that he's difficult to deal with.'

'Normally I wouldn't recommend writing this type of e-mail. Unless Freddy considers it completely necessary to explain his logic step by step or elaborate the previous discussion point for better understanding of the key issues, he should refrain from sending it, as it isn't going to accomplish anything productive.'

'Sure, e-mail can be used as an effective means of communication, but not in this context. Freddy is choosing an inappropriate way to get his point across to Trish. On the positive side, I'd say the content of his e-mail is overall quite good and well written, and it's good that he emphasizes his interest and personal commitment to make things work. He also raises informed views on the risks and explains why he believes things need to change. Finally, he concludes by proposing to discuss the issue more openly. On the negative side, venting one's own frustration in an e-mail is virtually never a good move, and I think that applies here. Best-case scenario is it gives Trish some food for thought. Worse-case scenario is that she sees it as a really poor move on Freddy's part.'

## 2. Fight the good fight – but be careful how you do it.

'I would have taken a different approach than the one Freddy took. I'd have tried to initiate a one-on-one conversation with Trish in order to solicit her thoughts and ask for her support directly, in person. You need to be able to judge someone's reaction to a request, especially if you're deciding to go up against management!'

'I think Freddy has the right idea in that he's not going to be able to move the needle by himself, but if there's low organizational or political capital available for him to do it, there's not much he can do … other than get his resume in shape.'

'I think, if Freddy is going to write an e-mail like this, he ought to think about it more and frame it better. I would have been more specific about my areas of disagreement and attempted to substantiate each of them very precisely. I also would have asked Trish to consider having a broader discussion with me about them, perhaps including others involved in the process. Then the ball would be in her court.'

'This is a risky strategy, and to even give it a chance of being successful, Freddy had better explain more specifically why he feels management's ideas will be counterproductive and divergent from the real purpose of the merger. I agree with his wanting to focus on the right goals and work within current management framework – I'm just saying he'd better have his ducks in a row, or else this could really backfire.'

3. **When trying to get others on your side, always consider what's at stake for them.**

'Freddy needs to think about Trish's perspective and position. I think she will probably do nothing with it, or maybe she'll send him a short reply saying something like, "I understand your concerns, but we discussed this yesterday and you heard the direction". Freddy needs to remember that he's asking Trish to spend some of her valuable political capital to advocate his argument. He needs to try to be smart about how much of that capital she is willing to spend on helping him.'

'I think that part of the big problem with an e-mail is that Freddy can get little to no sense of Trish's position. He doesn't know what she's thinking. There's a good chance here that he's going to be frustrated, discouraged or upset by her reaction.'

'Trish has the authority here. Freddy is asking her to take a flier for him, but does he really understand her personal goals or agenda? She might just ignore this completely and take the decision into her own hands now.'

'Based on previous discussions, it's hard to see Trish openly expressing disagreement with her superiors in management, so I imagine she will leave Freddy's e-mail unanswered, given that she's already tried once to clarify her alignment with management's view – or she might more abruptly let him know that he would be well advised to stick to what was agreed upon, and move on to another discussion!'

## Our Thoughts

In his original meeting with Trish and Vivian after getting promoted to his GM role, Freddy felt tongue-tied, unnerved and, following the meeting, as though he may have overstepped his bounds in his first hours on the job.

However, as a result of taking a risk and speaking up for the value orientation that he instinctively believed in, Freddy realized immediate benefits: the support of Trish in pursuing the value argument (in the form of performing an analysis of the potential Midwest acquisition); the encouragement of upper management in response to his analysis; and, ultimately, a prominent role in the merger itself.

Yet now, Freddy feels he is being pushed back several steps – perhaps all the way back to that first conversation, in which he found himself having to articulate, and defend, the value-creation line of reasoning to both his boss and his boss's boss, both of whom shared a conservative, short-term leaning. The difference now is that he and Trish are no longer debating it conceptually, but in practice, and that a crucial new element is now in play: the whims of those above her on the corporate hierarchy. Freddy must feel in part as though he was being 'strung along' by Trish and that she is now showing her true spots, or at least that, even if she agrees with his value standpoint in theory, when push comes to shove she does not truly have his back; nor does Vivian, who seems to cling even more strongly to a cautious, self-preserving approach.

Freddy does not seem the type who enjoys playing games or having to rely on strategic political manoeuvring. But it will serve him well at this point to remember that the long-term goal of value creation for the organization is just that – a *long-term* goal – and that there are numerous smaller steps toward achieving that goal. Those steps are not necessarily linear or unobstructed, and they must take place over time. No doubt Freddy is experiencing momentary frustration after perhaps developing the false sense that creating a company-wide value orientation was going to be a smooth, fast, 'all for one and one for all' process. The immediate situation is not only a trying one for Freddy, but also, more important, a concerning one, because of what it symbolizes to him: that different factions, with different outlooks, exist at Prism.

Eventually, he hopes that they will all stand for the same thing. He must accept the fact that, at least today, they do not. To be able to maintain his effectiveness, Freddy will require the skills of patience and tolerance. We use the word 'skills' because both can be practised and learned. If the value-based path forward is one of compromise, then Freddy needs to find a way of thinking, and communicating, that can get him through this period in a constructive, non-damaging way. It is possible, but deep personal awareness is required to make this work while still preserving a perception of fairness in the organization and maintaining one's own integrity.

**Your Thoughts**

## NANCY

### The Scenario

A day ago, Dana initiated a conversation with Nancy with the ostensible purpose of asking Nancy her impressions of the previous conversation in Calvin's office. Nancy tried to echo Calvin's message of remaining focused on value and putting aside personal opinions or feelings, but the conversation between the two women somehow deteriorated quickly, ending up as tense as their previous interactions. Nancy felt once again that Dana's style was both passive-aggressive and manipulative, and when Dana finally left her office, Nancy felt very frustrated, even though she felt she had done everything possible to encourage a mutually productive and neutral dialogue.

Nancy is now sitting at her desk when she receives an e-mail from Calvin requesting that she swing by his office at her earliest opportunity for 'a chat'. She receives the e-mail at 11:30 am.

Nancy e-mails back, 'Certainly. I just need to finish a few things and then will come by. How is 2:00?' In truth, Nancy has no work that she cannot temporarily defer, but she is trying to buy some time to think about, and prepare for, whatever Calvin may want to speak about.

Over the next two and a half hours, she comes no closer to figuring out Calvin's intentions. At 2:00, she nervously knocks on his office door. Here's how their conversation goes.

NANCY:   Good morning.
CALVIN:  Hi, Nancy. Please have a seat. How's your day going?
NANCY:   Fine, thanks.
CALVIN:  Great. Listen, I wanted to ask you how you feel your new role is going. You know, how you're handling everything.
NANCY:   Is this about Dana?
CALVIN:  It has nothing to do with Dana. I'm asking about you. How are you finding everything? I imagine this is a very different environment than the one you came from.

NANCY:    Yes, I suppose it is.

CALVIN:   You were with Whitesands for a decade. What was it like over there?

NANCY:    How do you mean?

CALVIN:   What was it like in terms of interaction? Collaboration? Did you spend most of your time at your desk doing work, or did you spend it mostly working with other folks in the organization?

NANCY:    Our department was pretty isolated, I suppose. I interacted a lot with my immediate supervisor, but the role was otherwise pretty individualized.

CALVIN:   And the other roles, as well?

NANCY:    For the most part, yes.

CALVIN:   Sounds pretty different from our situation here.

NANCY:    I guess that would be fair to say.

CALVIN:   How about the whole sugar-versus-steel thing? How do you feel about that? Does it affect you?

NANCY:    I don't think so. I mean, my role is one of Finance. The industries have similar elements, so …

CALVIN:   Your role is more than just Finance.

NANCY:    Hm?

CALVIN:   Nancy, for you to succeed at this level, it's important that you understand the requirements and implications of your role. It's very different from the one you had before. I want to help you get there, but I need you to be as open as possible. That means embracing input from others, and it means challenging yourself to see things in new ways.

NANCY:    I understand. I'm trying.

CALVIN:   I think you are trying. Let me ask you this. Was there much change in your other role at Whitesands over time?

NANCY:    No. My job stayed pretty static.

CALVIN:   And what about the company itself? Did you see a lot of change?

NANCY:    I would say no. It was mostly business as usual.

CALVIN:   I want you to leave that behind and get used to welcoming change instead. Change is learning, and we need to be learning continuously to succeed, because the marketplace changes continuously. Miguel was an effective CEO in some ways, but he also made single-minded decisions with a narrow, stubborn focus, and that's gotten us into the current trouble. We need to leave that kind of thinking behind. When I say your job isn't just a Finance one, I mean your job is the same as mine or anyone else's: to create ongoing value. Can you hear what I'm saying?

NANCY:    Yes, I hear it.

CALVIN:    Great. That's all for now. Thanks.

NANCY:    Thank you.

## Questions We Asked

1. In Nancy's position, how would you interpret what Calvin has said, and how he has said it?
2. Have you ever gone from one position, or company, to another where things were done very differently? How did you adjust?
3. Do you think Nancy will ultimately be successful in her role? Why or why not?

## Comments We Got

It could not have been more telling that all of our contributors' responses to the latest conversation between Calvin and Nancy centred around a single theme: the need for Nancy to heed Calvin's words once and for all. Most people admired Calvin's ongoing forbearance in the face of Nancy's seeming refusal to change, but most were also in strong agreement that he is issuing Nancy a clear warning at this juncture, and trying to make the same point in a different, more explicit way for her benefit. Calvin is not willing to give up on Nancy yet – but a number of our participants were.

### 1. It's about listening. And changing.

'It seems to me that Nancy is on thin ice. If I were her, I'd take Calvin's comments pretty seriously. The way I interpret them is that he doesn't think she's doing very well at fitting in or adapting to the scope her role demands, which is bigger than just

Finance. Calvin has repeatedly made comments to her about learning and changing. She needs to hear them.'

'Calvin is diplomatic and empathetic, but there is no mistaking his message to Nancy. She really needs to get that he is telling her she has a serious weakness – one that is not going to help the organization at a time when it needs leaders to drive change.'

'I think Calvin is basically telling Nancy she is getting one more chance to understand her expanded role and run with it. He reiterates the need for her to see, conceive and act on things that go beyond Finance. He tells her to think in terms of value and cross-functionality. He isn't mincing his words. She should be thankful for that, hear his message loud and clear, and do something about it.'

'Calvin refers to a person who was unable to change, failed in his role and contributed to the bad situation the company finds itself in. This is him giving Nancy an explicit signal about the imperative for her to change. He is trying to be very clear about the consequences of her refusing to change her attitude and behaviour. She needs to let down her guard and listen well to what he's trying to say.'

'I'd love to say that Nancy is going to become successful in her new role, but to be honest, at this point, it looks doubtful. She continues to spend a lot of time worrying about what her supervisor thinks of her, even though he's tried a lot to shift her thinking. At some point she needs to wake up and spend more time learning and trying to do her job well. That's what will show Calvin what he hopes to see.'

'It's difficult to be very optimistic about Nancy's trajectory given the rigidity she is showing. Her behaviour seems to demonstrate extreme resistance to the kind of change I think Calvin is asking of her.'

'I don't think Nancy is necessarily in denial of her own need for change, but her insecurity seems to be a major hurdle toward achieving it. Maybe she would have a better chance of success if she came to feel secure enough and "protected" by Calvin or the rest of the chain of command above her.'

'Nancy appears to have a long way to go before she embraces the mindset change necessary to succeed in her role. The danger is that the organization may not be willing to wait that long!'

## Our Thoughts

There is only one question following Calvin's brief meeting with Nancy in his office: will she recognize the import of what he is telling her?

Calvin has, for the most part, stopped mincing words. He has now elected to be more straight-ahead in his messaging to Nancy, a decision perhaps based on her apparent struggle to understand the intentions of previous discussions, whether including or excluding Dana. But he is also trying his best to convince her of the magnitude of the situation. Consider some of the phrases he uses:

'... for you to succeed at this level, it's important that you understand the requirements and implications of your role ...'

'I want to help you get there, but I need you to be as open as possible.'

'... embracing input from others ... challenging yourself to see things in new ways.'

'Change is learning, and we need to be learning continuously to succeed ...'

'... your job is the same as mine or anyone else's: to create ongoing value.'

If Nancy chooses to hear these words – and we sincerely hope she will – she still has a chance of turning her personal ship around. She can take heart that the five most important words Calvin has said to her during their talk are these: *'I think you are trying.'* He believes that she is making an effort to change.

Is she? The fact that she nervously tries to guess what he wants to talk about could be, if looked at charitably, a sign that she is at least invested in performing well at her role. We know that, at a minimum, she is not indifferent. No – Nancy's continuing problem is simply that Calvin's messages, at least thus far, have not gotten through to her, resulting in her sticking to an obstinate inward focus. Nancy must be willing to self-reflect and become more self-aware in order for her to be able to hear Calvin's, and others', messages. Her attitude and inability to take feedback are preventing her from making the shift in mindset to one of objectivity, openness to continuous learning and value-orientation for the organization. This shift is necessary in order for her to keep her current job. No boss is unendingly forgiving. Eventually, the decision will be made that Nancy cannot get on board. That decision isn't in the offing yet, but Calvin has painted a very clear picture at this point. The question is whether Nancy will choose to see it.

**Your Thoughts**

# HUGO

## The Scenario

*The previous day, Hugo called his boss Dino in frustration after trying futilely to compose an e-mail to his marketing team summarizing his positive endorsement of AMR's upcoming teddy bear rollout. The problem isn't that he is against the rollout, even though he has some instinctive reservations; it is that he is struggling to find the right way to frame his message to his team. As Hugo has discussed with Dino already, he now finds he is speaking a different language than they are, and though he has learned the importance of positioning his message as one of value creation, he wonders how it will be received by his group of marketers, who are driven by the same functional mentality he was just weeks ago.*

*Dino told Hugo he had to keep his head down for the rest of the day, and asked Hugo to come by the next day instead. Hugo knocks on Dino's office door. Dino is typing at his computer, responding to an e-mail. He gestures Hugo inside. Here's what transpires.*

HUGO:   Morning.
DINO:    Hey. Come on in. Just let me send this … and …
           *(Dino finishes typing and clicks Send.)*
           … done.
           *(Dino twirls his chair around to face Hugo.)*
DINO:    So. You feel like you're blowing it on both sides.
HUGO:   I feel like I've split into two people, and neither of them know exactly who they're supposed to be.
DINO:    You play golf?
HUGO:   A little.
DINO:    You know how, as soon as you fix one part of your swing, it creates two new problems you have to work on?
HUGO:   I am definitely familiar with that.
DINO:    This is kind of like that, my friend. Change is the only constant.
HUGO:   I buy the value message. Intellectually I understand the big picture, and our need to point the company in the right direction by making sound decisions. I'm completely in support of that. The

thing is, even though I get it, I feel like I'm not communicating it very well, or very consistently, either with my own team or the executive team.

DINO:    What's making you think that?

HUGO:    In my dealings with the other executives, I feel inadequate, and in my dealings with my own team, I feel … I don't know, just uncomfortable. Displaced.

DINO:    When were you promoted to this position?

HUGO:    About three weeks ago.

DINO:    Do you feel that's a long time?

HUGO:    No.

DINO:    You're a pretty driven guy, wouldn't you say?

HUGO:    Yes.

DINO:    You like to challenge yourself. Doing something successfully is important to you.

HUGO:    Yes, of course.

DINO:    You want to nail this thing. You want to do it right.

HUGO:    I want to do my job well – yes.

DINO:    And I admire that. It's a great benefit to the organization that you have that attitude. But this is a learning curve, and you're at the bottom. Probably feels a bit uncomfortable. I mean, you've spent, how many years in the company?

HUGO:    Fourteen.

DINO:    Fourteen years learning certain things, and now you're being told to forget them and open yourself to an entirely different, entirely new type of learning. The journey isn't always straight, you know what I mean?

HUGO:    No.

DINO:    I mean each new role doesn't build cleanly on the one before, like building blocks. Like I said, this job requires you to forget everything you learned in your last one, and the one before that, and the one before that. Not in terms of your skills and your knowledge, but personally. In terms of the dynamics with everyone else around you.

HUGO:    Yes. That's part of what I'm struggling with. But, also, I'd have to say, regarding the skills and knowledge I've spent so long developing – I feel like I don't exactly know how, or when, or in what proportion, to apply them.

DINO:    It will feel that way for a while.

HUGO:    And?

DINO:    And what?

HUGO:    I don't know, I was hoping you'd have something more … concrete to tell me.

DINO:    Nope. Keep doing what you're doing. You'll get there. Now go get some work done.

HUGO:    Okay. Thanks.

*(Hugo leaves Dino's office, somewhat befuddled.)*

## Questions We Asked

1. How do you feel Hugo is doing in his transition to his new role as GM?
2. Do you feel Dino is giving Hugo the right kind of guidance for him to be able to progress?
3. Have you ever been in a position where you were given some basic guidance in a new role but mostly had to figure it out on your own? How did you feel, and how did it go?

## Comments We Got

The majority of our participants have had it with Hugo – in a good way. They appreciate his positive attitude, his continued willingness to learn and his sincere attempts to internalize Dino's teachings. Now, they want him to seize the reins and truly dive in. They want him to self-accelerate. They want him not to be satisfied with a basic understanding of value creation, but to push himself deeper into the weeds. They feel he has gained a sufficient amount of confidence and a broad enough foundation to take bigger steps forward at this point, for his own benefit, the benefit of his team and, most important, the long-term health of AMR.

Numerous members of the participant community suggested that a mentoring counterpart to Dino might be of great help to Hugo moving forward. Dino has been invaluable to Hugo in gaining a sense of self-assurance, and a baseline understanding of the value perspective. The other element that Hugo is sorely in need of, most agree, is true leadership. The group is somewhat sceptical over whether Dino can light the proper leadership fire under Hugo. Our participants are confident that he can walk him through the general manager's strategic toolkit, but if there is one very obvious area in which Hugo falls short, it is in his lacking communication skills, weak personality and hesitating manner. Someone to complement Dino's more concrete approach, many suggested, might be the right missing piece to help vault Hugo to the next level, allowing him not only to understand and live the value-creation approach himself, but also to communicate it properly and persuasively to others.

Contributors' overall responses converged around two separate themes. Here they are, plus some of the more representative comments.

## 1. Learn steadily, but not slowly.

'I think Hugo is trying, but he still seems like a real fish out of water. It just seems very difficult for him to let go of his old self – that is, his old role, and the expertise that got him here, but won't keep him here.'

'I wouldn't say Hugo is doing so bad. He is aware of his strengths and weaknesses and feels secure enough to expose these and to seek guidance, which is after all half the battle.'

'I like that Hugo is trying to identify ways to leverage his experience and grow progressively in his new role, even if he isn't finding it so easy right away. He is asking himself an important question: "Who am I supposed to be in this new context?" Asking himself the question is good. I think he's having a difficult time finding the answer.'

'To me, Hugo is still confused, and he is not doing well leading his team or contributing at the level of management. To his credit, though, I think he does sincerely listen to what Dino has to say, and you can't question his effort or desire. I would give him the benefit of the doubt. It seems like just a matter of time.'

'Hugo has taken in a lot of learning in three weeks, but I wonder whether he is putting it into practice quickly enough. Dino is very patient with him, but how long will it last?'

## 2. Seek help along the way.

'Perhaps at this point Hugo could ask a different senior executive – not Dino – to be his mentor so he can accelerate his own learning process, which he seems to be struggling with. He could also ask for some special training on leadership or other areas in which he is weak, like finance. Come on Hugo, we love you!'

'Hugo is seeking technical, mechanistic advice from Dino, but I think he also needs true leadership inspiration. That, to me, may make the difference for him. It's great that he is getting nuts-and-bolts guidance from Dino, but I'm not sure he seems properly motivated as a GM.'

'Dino did mention that Hugo is on the steep part of a learning curve, and that he must continue to learn. But I think Dino is trying to nudge him along slowly, whereas perhaps it might be more effective to push him to jump into the job with both feet.'

'I think I would use a different approach with Hugo. I'd tell him that his job for the next 90 days is to learn and digest as much as he possibly can. He needs to become a student of the business and the role, and to try to build a mental business model for success to every extent he can. This means spending quality one-to-one time with as many relevant stakeholders as possible, both above and below him. It is hard to move up the learning curve without the right tools, and the right relationships to help you do it.'

'I give Dino points for guiding Hugo with a healthy balance. He provides him hints about his strengths (willingness to get things done well and in the "right" way) and also tells him about his need to change (such as, but not limited to, avoiding applying the same skills he did in his previous role). Hugo always seems to leave the discussions with Dino thoughtful, motivated, entrusted and put at ease.'

'No one ever gave me advice on my new role. I had to define it for myself.'

'It can be really uncomfortable trying to slip comfortably into such a new, different role, and I believe Dino is helping Hugo a lot in this regard. I think Dino understands the difficulty Hugo is experiencing, and that he requires a lot of briefing and coaching in order to ultimately succeed. Dino is giving Hugo a mental workplan while challenging and engage him to seek definition for his role and himself.'

'When I moved into a new role, I got very little guidance on what I was supposed to be doing. I spent a lot of time talking with others, asking their thoughts on how they viewed my role and what it was meant to contribute. It helped.'

'Throwing yourself into the role and the internal network is a good way to become immediately visible and therefore get the benefit of immediate help from others. When you show you are welcome to learning and change, those around you want to step up and help. I did this, and found that everyone I spoke with was very willing to provide coaching or guidance. Once I got up to speed and figured out who I needed to work with to get things done, I had already built up the relationships and knowledge to make it much easier.'

## Our Thoughts

Hugo has every chance to make his management journey a success. His greatest areas of need are obvious, and his progress may at times seem a bit slow. But it is better that he asks constant questions and seeks ongoing guidance than if he were to believe at this point that he is a fully formed GM whose transformation is complete, and who has now learned everything he needs to learn.

'Keep doing what you're doing,' Dino tells Hugo, and he is right. He is telling him to continue asking questions even when the answers seem elusive. He is telling him to continue learning as much as possible, rather than fretting over how he is executing the duties of the position. Dino reminds Hugo that he has been at his new post only a few weeks, after coming up through the functional ranks of marketing for nearly a decade and a half. That, Dino reminds Hugo, is a lot of unlearning. In effect, Hugo is being pushed and encouraged, by the new role and by his boss, to develop a level of comfort with the ambiguity of his new role, and with the need for continuous learning, without arriving at conclusive knowledge or answers, while simultaneously embracing the use of data to support or refute any claim to knowledge.

Hugo has grown more and more receptive to the idea that he must abandon everything that has brought him to this point and now work from a fresh mindset and an evolved practical framework. He continues to make slow but steady progress forward, even if that progress is represented mostly by his admitting that he doesn't have the answers.

**Your Thoughts**

\*    \*    \*

## Overall Discussion

If it's true that change is the only constant, our three GMs are living proof. They are each, in different ways, coming to grips with the fact that their management journey has only just begun. During this journey, they have arrived at certain critical realizations, from a basic grasp of the value-based perspective, to the importance of focusing on objective data, to the difference between the usefulness of knowledge and experience on one hand and the hazard of bias and opinion on the other. Not only do the questions they face continue to change, but the answers seem to be constantly changing as well.

It is imperative that our GMs see this constant change as an opportunity rather than an impediment. In embracing the early stages of their management transformation, they are hopefully taking a crucial step by understanding that their own journey toward self-awareness begins by acknowledging that they don't have the answers, yet that in not having the answers, they must often provide them anyway, at least in the form of guiding questions and refinement of responses using data and logic.

They have embraced, to varying degrees, the value perspective. They have made every effort to understand it in theory, and also what it means in practice. They have done their best to get comfortable with finance and confront other issues that previously lay safely outside their functional comfort zones. In the end, they have come face to face with the most important fact of all: that their own internal transformation must take place before any external change can occur, and that, even in the face of their own success, there is room to do better.

They have discovered that they occupy a role of great flexibility, great importance and great potential, and that they can serve as vital facilitators of value to help their organizations make decisions today that contribute to a sustainable future. At the end of their leadership journey, what have our GMs learned? Hopefully that they aren't at the end of their journey at all, but the beginning.

## Key Questions to Ask Yourself

1. What mechanism or trick do you use to make sure you don't accidentally undermine your effectiveness or, worse, do long-term damage to your reputation and career, when you temporarily succumb to your emotions (e.g. you want to lash out at an underperforming member of the team, send a scathing e-mail to vent frustration, etc.)?

2. Are you able to continuously dig deep within your conscious and subconscious motivations to recognize when they are leading you astray? What devices do you employ to make these self-checks on a regular basis?

3. As you recognize the unending ambiguity in general management, are you able to find confidence in your own mental processes and your approach to new questions, rather than needing answers to the questions in order to feel confident in the role? Are you comfortable building a leadership and communication style around a new form of expertise that increasingly entails asking the right questions instead of having the right answers?

# A Final Word

We hope that, as you vicariously reach the conclusions of the journeys taken by Freddy, Nancy and Hugo, you have gained some insight into the journey you yourself are on. Each organization is different, each individual passage unique, and each career evolution its own particular animal, but if we have made any point, we hope it is this: you are now part of something bigger. You are in the midst of becoming a more active and influential agent in a vital endeavour: no less than the effort to help ensure your company's future growth and success.

Your personal and professional transition will look different from anyone else's. You have your own personality, your own background, your own biases, your own skill set, your own hot buttons and blind spots. Our goal in writing this book is not to prescribe any one formula for success. Rather, it is to highlight the importance of the change you must undergo to step effectively into this new role. It is not an overnight transition; it takes time, effort and willingness.

You have watched our three fictional characters take some of the early steps in this change. We hope that the scenarios in which they have found themselves speak to some of your own experiences, and moreover that the ways in which they have handled these situations, both good and bad, and both the commentary from our contributors and the input we provided, have produced some insights into your individual journey.

The path you are on does not take place in a vacuum. We encourage you to leverage those around you, seek guidance from those who have experience and those you trust, and open yourself up to as much learning and skill-building as you can. Freddy, Nancy and Hugo have each come to understand that the functional competence that got them to where they are must now be replaced by a whole new suite of abilities, from managing agendas and expectations above and below, to finding new ways to communicate, to developing proficiency with finance. At certain points, they have been accepting of this realization; at other times, they have been resistant. Ultimately, all three must thrust themselves fully into this new realm of learning and discovery to become the sound decision-makers and effective contributors of value those above them believe they can be.

The successful journey to general management, of course, is not only about acquiring new professional skills. If the stories of Freddy, Nancy and Hugo teach us anything, it is that the types of changes required to thrive at this level are in large part internal. It is not just the learning that matters, but the willingness to admit the need for learning. It is not just the acquisition of new abilities, but the readiness to virtually abandon the ones that got you this far. It is not just a matter of adjusting your viewpoint slightly, but a matter of embracing a new perspective altogether. Our three GMs have shown us that the passage into this new territory demands of them three separate but interrelated tasks. They must manage the business; they must manage others; and, above all, they must manage themselves. The stories and observations of others only reinforce this truth.

We wish you the best in your own management journey.

**Kevin Kaiser, Michael Pich and I.J. Schecter**

# About the Website

The videos discussed in *Becoming a Top Manager* can be viewed at **www.wiley.com/go/topmanager**, using the password 'kaiser321'. This website also contains other materials and interactive tools which we encourage you to take advantage of as you go through your own management journey. We would be pleased to receive, and respond to, your comments and stories.

# About the Authors

Professor of Management Practice at INSEAD and Director of its Transition to General Management programme, **Kevin Kaiser** is former Adjunct Professor of Finance at Kellogg School of Management, Northwestern University, as well as a former member of McKinsey & Company's Corporate Finance and Strategy practice. Professor Kaiser is co-author, with fellow INSEAD instructor S. David Young, of *The Blue Line Imperative: What Managing for Value Really Means*.

Dean of Executive Education at INSEAD, **Michael Pich** focuses on ensuring that the programme portfolio provides transformational learning experiences for both individuals and businesses. Prior to his appointment as Dean, Professor Pich was a Senior Affiliate Professor in Operations Management, and Entrepreneurship and Family Enterprise. Professor Pich directed INSEAD's flagship Transition to General Management programme for its first decade.

Former McKinsey & Company communications specialist, **I.J. Schecter** is an award-winning author and journalist and CEO of

The Schecter Group, a leading global communications firm helping Fortune 500 companies like Visa, Coca-Cola and CitiGroup shape their voices, craft their messages and tell their stories. Mr. Schecter is author, co-author or ghostwriter of multiple bestselling business titles over the past decade.

# Index